More Praise for *One Piece of Paper*

"With his unique insights from decades of experience as a combat arms officer, management consultant, Fortune 500 executive, and entrepreneur, Mike Figliuolo has hit the mark with a must-read for leaders at all levels who want to radically improve their effectiveness."
—The Honorable David McCormick, Under Secretary of the U.S. Treasury (2007–2009)

"Once I began it, I could not put Mike's book down as I learned how to learn about myself. Beginning with establishing an honest, personal introspective foundation, *One Piece of Paper* provides a hands-on, actionable guide to credible, effective leadership."
—Jack Partridge, president, Columbia Gas of Ohio, Inc.

"Dynamic leaders at all levels will benefit from Mike Figliuolo's experience and powerful approach. If you are ready to take ownership of defining your authentic style of leadership, then *One Piece of Paper* is the place to begin."
—Kim Gravell, vice president, Strategy Management, Cardinal Health

"*One Piece of Paper* is exceptionally framed, forward-thinking, and thought provoking. Mike Figliuolo provides key leadership insights and perspectives that are real. This book represents concise, practical, and effective thinking on leadership, and plainly said, this approach works."
—Darcie Zeliesko, group leader, Heinz North America

"Mike Figliuolo's maxims approach to leadership provides a simple yet profound template for developing the kind of synergy, trust, and confidence essential for successful organizations."
—Robert F. Foley, Lieutenant General, U.S. Army, Retired

ONE PIECE
OF PAPER

ONE PIECE OF PAPER

[THE SIMPLE APPROACH TO
POWERFUL, PERSONAL LEADERSHIP]

MIKE FIGLIUOLO

JOSSEY-BASS
A Wiley Imprint
www.josseybass.com

Published by Jossey-Bass
A Wiley Imprint
989 Market Street, San Francisco, CA 94103-1741—www.josseybass.com

Jossey-Bass books and products are available through most bookstores. To contact Jossey-Bass directly call our Customer Care Department within the U.S. at 800-956-7739, outside the U.S. at 317-572-3986, or fax 317-572-4002.

Wiley also publishes its books in a variety of electronic formats and by print-on-demand. Some material included with standard print versions of this book may not be included in e-books or in print-on-demand. If the version of this book that you purchased references media such as CD or DVD that was not included in your purchase, you may download this material at http://booksupport.wiley.com. For more information about Wiley products, visit www.wiley.com.

Library of Congress Cataloging-in-Publication Data

Figliuolo, Mike, 1970-
  One piece of paper : the simple approach to powerful, personal leadership / Mike Figliuolo. — 1st ed.
     p. cm.
  Includes index.
  ISBN 978-1-118-04959-4 (hardback), 978-1-118-12337-9 (ebk), 978-1-118-12338-6 (ebk), 978-1-118-12339-3 (ebk)
  1. Leadership. 2. Leadership—Philosophy. I. Title.
  HM1261.F54 2011
  303.3'4—dc23

                             2011025737

Printed in the United States of America
FIRST EDITION

HB Printing   V10004545_091318

To Danielle, Michael, and Alexandra.
Nothing is beyond your reach. Don't let the world
define you. You define your world.

To Nana. Thank you for your love, laughs, and
for teaching me many of the principles in this book.
You'll always be missed and never forgotten.

CONTENTS

PART FOUR   LEADING YOUR PEOPLE

PART FIVE   LEADING A BALANCED LIFE

PART SIX   MAKING IT REAL

ONE PIECE
OF PAPER

THE LEADERSHIP MAXIMS APPROACH

CHAPTER 1

[UNDERSTANDING THE LEADERSHIP MAXIMS APPROACH]

Imagine being able to explain your leadership philosophy on one piece of paper—a simple 8.5- by 11-inch summation of all you are and all you want to be as a leader. How powerful would it be to have a discussion about that single page with the members of your team? They would be thrilled to have just one page to read, understand, and internalize. Envision how that one page could simplify and clarify how you want your team members to conduct themselves. Think about how impressed candidates and new hires would be if they could quickly understand your standards, expectations, and goals easily and from one single solitary page.

I have had the privilege of working with leaders at companies large and small across many industries, functions, and levels, and the one major commonality across that broad range of experience is the challenge they face—how to clearly, succinctly articulate who they are as leaders, and then lead according to that individual leadership philosophy on a daily basis. There is no shortage of great thinking on leadership, but the *application* of those thoughts to everyday leadership situations is challenging, especially in corporate environments.

The study of leadership can be daunting. There are massive tomes written on the subject. It is taught in universities and MBA programs. Entire fields of study are dedicated to leadership. Companies create massive corporate programs and universities to foster it in their associates. Yet despite all that, leaders in the trenches still find it difficult to define their own personal style of leadership. It seems even harder to master the day-to-day application of the leadership philosophy they espouse.

Here's the thing—it's really not that hard. Leadership is an intensely personal sport. Every leader is different. But one thing all leaders have in common is the need to understand, articulate, and continuously improve their leadership philosophy and do so in a simple, straightforward way.

We have difficulty nailing down our leadership philosophies because we focus too much on the output of the process (a leadership philosophy) and not enough on understanding how to generate that output. This fixation on output leads us to produce cookie-cutter constructs for what a "good" leadership philosophy looks like. Leaders develop the mindset *If my philosophy doesn't look like the philosophies of other leaders, it must be wrong.* With that mindset, leaders end up constructing philosophies that are eerily similar to those of every other leader around them. Leaders who do this become followers under that approach, and the resulting philosophies tend to use excessive amounts of jargon and buzzwords. Those kinds of philosophies reveal nothing about the personality or true beliefs of the leader and therefore do little to establish a trust-based relationship between the leader and the led. When leaders follow a philosophy that is not truly their own, it can cause them to act like someone they are not; if they claim to believe in such a philosophy but stay true to themselves, they can end up behaving in ways that are inconsistent with the philosophy they profess to follow. These inconsistencies can create confusion and mistrust between the leaders and their teams.

The leadership maxims approach reverses that dynamic. It acknowledges a simple truth—people are complex and multidimensional. It states that *the method* for defining one's leadership philosophy is common to all leaders but *the output* of that process is as varied as the shapes of snowflakes. By accepting that your philosophy can and should be dramatically different from those of others, you free yourself from artificial buzzwords, and you avoid the meaningless corporate-speak everyone can see through in an instant. The leadership maxims approach helps you articulate who you really are as a leader versus who you think the organization wants you to be. This consistency between the leader's philosophy and actions builds trust among the leader and his team and reduces confusion about the leader's expectations and standards. When this occurs, the team can focus on their jobs rather than wasting time and energy trying to figure out their leader.

What I am going to share with you can be your leadership secret (although as part of the process you are expected to share this secret with others). I have personally used and taught this approach for years, and it has been a powerful tool for improving myself and my performance. My own perspective has been informed by my experiences in the military, as a management consultant, as a manager and executive in large companies, and as a leadership trainer and coach. I have worked in multiple industries including financial services, pharmaceuticals, consumer goods, chemicals, health care, technology, academia, and retail. My experiences have spanned many functional areas, from call centers to corporate strategy, and I have worked with leaders at all levels, from frontline managers to senior executives and CEOs.

The approach outlined in this book will help you to clarify, for yourself and others, the heart of your personal leadership philosophy, and to do so simply enough that you can capture it on a single piece of paper. As you apply this method, you will write down fifteen to twenty emotionally powerful statements or reminders of personal events that will serve to guide your behaviors on a daily basis.

To get a complete view of your leadership philosophy, you need to evaluate four aspects of leadership:

- *Leading yourself:* what motivates you and what are your rules of personal conduct? What do you want "future you" to look like and stand for?
- *Leading the thinking:* where are you taking the organization and how will you innovate to drive change? What are your standards of performance for how you will safely get to your destination?
- *Leading your people:* how can you lead them as individuals rather than treating them like faceless cogs in the machine?
- *Leading a balanced life:* if you are burned out, you are worthless. How do you define and achieve balance?

All four aspects of leadership are equally important. Many leadership models focus exclusively on leading your people. That happens because it is easy to conceptualize leadership in a basic leader-led construct. Strategy and innovation models emphasize leading the thinking. Self-help models target leading yourself. And in the frantic pace of today's environment, leading a balanced life often falls by the wayside. Each aspect of leadership is important in its own right, but focusing on one to the exclusion of others creates imbalance. If you try to understand and build your capabilities in all four aspects of leadership but study them independently of one another, you risk creating a leadership philosophy full of inconsistencies. Even if you are able to make the precepts of your philosophy consistent, you still run the risk of that philosophy being confusing. This could happen because you will have cobbled together multiple frameworks and approaches. Those frameworks are not necessarily designed to work well with the tools and frameworks contained in other theories pertaining to the other aspects of leadership. The result is a philosophy that pieces together interesting components from multiple approaches but it does not actually fit together in a way that is consistent or compelling. If you truly want your philosophy to be well-constructed, the tools you use should all come from the same toolbox. This book is that toolbox.

CREATING YOUR MAXIMS

A maxim by definition is a principle or rule of conduct. In the context of the leadership maxims approach, it is a short, personally meaningful, and easily explained statement that reflects one of your beliefs about leadership. Maxims do not contain buzzwords (like *leverage, optimize, outside the box, win-win*). Maxims are simple, clear statements that serve as reminders for how you want to behave and lead and how you want your team members to behave. When written well, your leadership maxims become simple daily reminders of how you should behave so your actions are consistent with who you want to be as a leader. Your maxims will become your leadership conscience. They will help you make difficult decisions and choose paths consistent with the kind of leader you aspire to be.

Maxims must be emotionally meaningful, so you need to delve into your personal experiences to find those phrases, images, and stories that stir you to your core. By having your maxims elicit an emotional and physical reaction, the likelihood that they will change your behavior is exponentially higher than if you try rallying to a string of meaningless buzzwords. Maxims can be found in painful lessons you have experienced and distilled down to their essence. They can also be drawn from incredibly positive experiences. They can be inspiring song lyrics. They can be images that stand for something you find deeply important. They can be sayings used by family members, teachers, or coaches that hold significant meaning, or quotes from a book or memories that serve as reminders of powerful leadership stories you have experienced. Maxims can come from anywhere or anything. The most important attributes of maxims are that they are clear, pithy, and personally meaningful. By being short and direct, the maxim is easy to remember and access. By being personally meaningful, the maxim elicits a powerful emotional response that leads to behavior change. By being from your own experience, the maxim serves as a vehicle to share your stories with your team and strengthen the bonds of understanding and trust you have with them.

Articulating your maxims requires a process of introspection. You need to answer questions pertaining to each of the four aspects of leadership and use those questions to define your personal approach to leadership in that arena. For this to work, your answers must be open and honest; that is what makes your maxims authentic and easily understood by those around you. The synthesis of your answers into emotionally compelling and resonant statements will serve as the foundation for your leadership philosophy. Your answers will eventually become your personal leadership maxims.

At first, this process may feel awkward. Too often we are taught not to share personal things at the office. Over the years, this mindset can make us stuffy and render our emotions inaccessible. We may build up a defensive veneer of corporate propriety that is difficult to penetrate, and our true selves can be pushed down. Breaking down these barriers can be painful and takes a lot of energy. Your first few attempts at writing a maxim will probably be odd, because there is a good chance you are not used to accessing your emotions in a structured and focused way. You will likely start the process by writing something that sounds good but means nothing. It will be some universal truth no one can argue with, like "I will continuously add value to the organization." Don't believe me? Write your first few maxims, then wait a couple of weeks. Go back and reread what you wrote. Is it meaningful? Does it resonate to your core? Do those words move you to action? Do they say something about you as an individual? You may be surprised and disappointed by your answers to these questions.

Once you do have a complete set of maxims that you are happy with—and trust me, if you make the effort, you *can* do this—you will have created a leadership philosophy reflective of who you are as a whole person. Doing this does require you to evaluate all four aspects of leadership at the same time. Through this evaluation, you will build internal consistency in your philosophy by understanding and articulating how the four aspects of leadership relate to one another. A maxim you create for how you will lead yourself must make sense in the context of how you lead a balanced life. The way you lead the thinking will influence the maxims you define for how you lead your people. Building this consistency and these linkages across these four aspects of leadership will strengthen your entire leadership philosophy.

The all-encompassing nature of your leadership maxims provides you a means for living your leadership philosophy during every waking moment of your existence. It is that constant application of your leadership maxims that strengthens the leader you are and will become. Theory is nice. *Application* is where you have an impact on the world around you.

APPLYING YOUR MAXIMS

As you apply your maxims on a regular basis, your behaviors will become more predictable for your team members, colleagues, friends, and family. That predictability and consistency are the foundation of trust for all your relationships. You can achieve consistency through the maxims approach first, because you have written your maxims down as rules you'd like to live by and second, because you have shared those maxims with others. That sharing strengthens your accountability for living up to those standards. As a simple example, imagine you tell yourself you are going to swear off cookies and lose five pounds. If you do not tell another soul about your no-cookie rule or your goal, how susceptible will you be to breaking your rule when you see that brand new box of double-stuffed cream-filled cookies in the pantry? I am pretty sure if you are anything like me you will pour yourself a tall, cold glass of milk and dig in. But what if you've told everyone in your family about your goal and your no-cookie rule? You are more likely to adhere to that rule, because now you are not only letting yourself down by not following it, but you also are showing your weakness to other people you care about. Many of us can accept letting ourselves down, but letting down others we care about stings a great deal. Sharing your maxims with people you care about is a powerful reinforcing technique for making your desired behaviors stick.

Your maxims are a reflection of your leadership beliefs at a given point in time. They will change as you grow and have new experiences or deal with different leadership situations. By virtue of understanding and accepting the evolving nature of your maxims, you are committing to regular introspection and reevaluation of your leadership philosophy as the world around you changes and you find yourself in new circumstances. The constant evolution of your maxims makes them more powerful every day. The dynamic nature of maxims creates an environment in which you are continuously improving your skills as a leader.

I unwittingly stumbled upon and used the leadership maxims approach when I was a young platoon leader in the army. When I took over my unit, I unsuccessfully tried to explain to my soldiers what I believed in as a leader. I failed because the concepts I articulated were full of jargon but devoid of meaning. Eventually I began telling them "I have two expectations of you, and you can have the same two expectations of me: work hard and be honest. That's it. If we all do those two things, I can't ask anything more, and we'll succeed at whatever we're doing."

It clicked. Those two simple expectations resonated. They were deeply meaningful for me. They were easily understood by others. We could evaluate every daily action against those two principles and quickly determine whether we had lived up to that standard or not. My soldiers and I used them on a regular basis, and they helped drive behavior and set standards both for ourselves and for each other. My leadership maxims were born.

The maxims approach requires you to share your life experiences with others, which can be very difficult. Many of those experiences may have been painful, or you may consider some of them too personal. The thought of sharing these stories with people you don't know well can prompt all sorts of uncomfortable thoughts. *What if someone makes fun of me? What if they think I'm weak because I cry at the end of* Old Yeller? *Will they still respect me if they know I struck out in kickball in third grade?* These nagging doubts and fears are the barrier between you and authenticity. Those fears lead you to erect walls that keep others out and keep your emotions in. If, however, you tear down these walls, you humanize yourself. You become less intimidating as a boss. People will see you not as an emotionless instrument of the machine, but as *you*, in all your imperfect glory—and they will respect you for it. They will be more likely to trust you because you have shared personal truths about yourself with them.

Allow me to demonstrate. I once struck out playing kickball in third grade. Not that I was extremely uncoordinated as a kid; I was simply having a bad day. Three pitches. Three mighty swings of a Converse-covered right foot. Three colossal whiffs. It was humiliating. The laughter was deafening, and I thought I was going to die from embarrassment. That game happened thirty years ago, so now I am able to simply laugh at that strikeout. Sure, it still smarts a bit when I first remember that moment, but time and perspective have eased that pain, and I have taken away a lesson from it. There have been instances since that strikeout when I have done something embarrassing and others have laughed, but instead of wallowing in the pain of being laughed at, I have instead touched on a personal maxim: *We all strike out at kickball once.* Doing so reminds me that no matter how hard people are laughing at me for something, at some point the laughter stops and life continues.

Sharing your maxims and the stories that go along with them is humanizing. It will help your colleagues empathize with you, and if they can empathize with you, they can connect with and relate to you. This helps build the respect and understanding necessary for developing an interpersonal relationship. All you have to do to make that connection is share something personal. In my case, I had to overcome my fear of being laughed at and tell my colleagues I'd struck out at kickball. By doing this, I was implicitly telling them I trusted them not to mock me when I shared my story. That first extension of trust begins building our relationships with one another.

Your first attempts to examine your past will likely be stilted and guarded. You may have repressed your emotions for a long time without realizing it. True feelings of joy, pain, fear, triumph, and excitement are lurking below a crust of professionalism, maturity, and insecurity, and breaking through those layers is hard work. The good news is, the more comfortable you get with the approach, the more personal your maxims will become. Including your personal story as the foundation for your maxims is the key to successfully articulating a leadership philosophy that will help you build powerful relationships and serve people, yourself included, as a courageous leader.

As you follow the maxims method to the end, you will find your maxims flow more and more easily. You will become more comfortable sharing who you really are as a person. Again, after you finish going through the process once and then go back to reread the first maxims you wrote, you may be disappointed in yourself. You may see stoicism and cynicism holding your emotions back in those first few maxims. But as you keep reading your work, you will see a tremendous difference in how much you have shared about yourself in writing your later maxims. You are learning how to access your feelings. Remember— your maxims are a living document. Once you realize how cold and unemotional your first few maxims are, you can revise them, infusing them with the richness of your experience. It is only once you finally get over your emotional hang-ups and decide to put yourself out there in a way that exposes who you truly are that you can make the leap into authentic leadership. The maxims approach is your bridge over that gaping void we mistakenly call leadership in our too-often cold, emotionless business world. Once you are on the other side, you will understand how powerful you can be as an imperfect and genuine leader.

THE BENEFITS OF THE LEADERSHIP MAXIMS APPROACH

The leadership maxims approach has many benefits. First, your maxims will help you set aspirational goals to be a better leader and to continue your personal and professional growth. Second, your maxims will set expectations for your team members for how you want them to behave.

These expectations reduce confusion and inefficiency stemming from the perennial question *What's on the boss's mind today?* Third, your maxims will help you and your team members make better decisions more rapidly, because you will have an established set of principles for how you want to behave as a leader and how you want them to behave as members of your team. These principles will be defined during times of calm and introspection. They will be used in times of chaos and confusion. When those times of chaos arrive, you can simply rely on a predefined rule of conduct and make what you know will be a good decision because it is consistent with previously articulated values. You will no longer have to hold multiple meetings and evaluate all possible choices before you can make a decision with which you are comfortable.

If you are serious about trying a new approach to leadership and you are committed to writing your own set of maxims, you need to think of this as a workbook, not a "reading book." The rest of this book is divided into five parts. The following four parts cover the four aspects of leadership: leading yourself, leading the thinking, leading your people, and leading a balanced life. The fifth part covers how you can put your maxims into action on a regular basis so they can begin changing your behavior and the behaviors of your team. In each of the leadership aspect sections I will explain that aspect, then guide you through a series of pointed questions related to that aspect. As you read those questions, I will share how other leaders and I used them to guide the creation of one of our personal leadership maxims. I have shared my personal maxim for every set of questions in this book, to provide an example of how one person can go through these exercises and create their own maxims, as well as to give you a sense for how, when done well, the resulting set of maxims paints a complete picture of one individual leader. You will see how my maxims reinforce one another and how the combined set of maxims provides a consistent view of what my teams can expect from me as a leader. In many sections I have also provided examples of maxims generated by other leaders. These examples, from leaders in different industries, functions, countries, and levels of organizations, will give you a sense of how broadly applicable the method is while at the same time how very different the resulting maxims can be for different individuals. After you read our stories and maxims, you will write a maxim of your own and document it in the appendix of this book.

Don't worry—I will provide plenty of guidance, suggestions, and ideas on how you can create your maxims. When you have worked through all four aspects of leadership and answered each associated question, you will have created your first draft of your own personal leadership maxims. Going through this process will require significant effort on your part, but I think you will learn a great deal about yourself and your approach to leadership along the way, and you will find those insights tremendously satisfying. I will ask you to be thoughtful and to share personal stories about yourself you may never have shared before. I promise that if you approach this work thoughtfully, bravely, and authentically you will end up with a powerful leadership document that will guide you, your team, your decisions, and your behaviors for many years to come.

Leadership takes effort, but the practice itself should not be exceedingly complex. The key to great leadership is knowing who you are as a leader and who you want to be, and being rigorous in how you define those beliefs in a compelling yet accessible way. Some of you may be thinking *Wrong! Leadership is about the actions you take!* I agree that actions matter, but you are a step ahead of yourself. Allow me to ask you this— on what basis will you decide whether an action is a good one or a bad one? Without a clear leadership philosophy, taking action is dangerous. Yes, you have innate beliefs that guide your actions. I am asking you to make those beliefs *explicit*. The process of defining and articulating the beliefs that guide your actions is the leadership maxims approach.

Now, I invite you to embark on that journey of understanding who you are as a leader, who you want to be, and how you would like to get there. You are going to define your entire leadership philosophy— on one piece of paper.

CHAPTER 2

[ON BUZZWORDS]

If you have been in the professional world for more than a year, you have probably heard something like this countless times:

> My leadership philosophy is to optimally leverage the passions of my people such that at the end of the day we maximize employee engagement to get them to think outside the box and synergistically drive value-added activities in a profit-maximizing way that is a win-win for our people, our shareholders, and our customers.

It sounds great. It is polysyllabic. It uses words with long definitions. I have only one question: What the hell does it mean?

Think of this chapter as a palate cleanser. I want you to wipe away all those unproductive phrases and words that get in the way of your being an authentic leader. Consider this a bit of a slap upside the head. You may not realize how deeply ingrained some bad behaviors have become in your daily routine. You have likely looked on the world through the same lens for a while, and that lens colors the way you view leadership. The color of that lens is determined largely by your organization's culture. Somewhere along the way that culture has shaped you more than you are shaping it. We are going to reverse that dynamic. Leaders should determine the culture of their organizations—not the other way around. Sure, leaders have to operate within their given organizational culture, but they do not have to succumb to its tendency to create drones and sacrifice their personality to it. Some aspects of culture are good. Others, well, not so much. I have noticed over the years that many organizational cultures lead people to articulate ideas in a less-than-genuine way. In other words, we end up using buzzwords that, if left unchecked, turn into bullshit.

Corporate-speak is pervasive. Buzzwords have insidiously worked their way into normal conversations. The use of such language obscures truth and meaning. When people hear it, some are impressed and initially believe you have said something meaningful and insightful. Upon further reflection, however, they usually realize you have not told them anything. All you have done is confuse and frustrate them. Unfortunately, people will rarely push hard for clarification of the true meaning behind all those words. Why? Because they are embarrassed to ask for an explanation. If they ask you to explain what you mean by all that jargon, they expose themselves to ridicule. They may fear that everyone will think they are stupid because they cannot decode the brilliant insights locked up in that string of gigantic words. Instead of asking for clarification, they simply nod as if they understand, then slink away to their desks, confused.

Let's make this situation worse—imagine you are the boss using all the big confusing words and the confused person is a member of your team. How likely is that team member to say *Hey boss, that sounds great, but you're not making any sense. Can you use real words and simply tell us what you want us to do?* Not likely, right? Now reverse the situation. Imagine you are the employee and your boss is the one spewing the endless stream of buzzwords. How excited are you to follow that person? I would venture to guess your answer is "not very," mostly because you are not sure where the person is trying to lead you.

The worst part is that these buzzwords have migrated from corporate strategy and consultant presentations into how we talk about ourselves as leaders. We are taught that all good leaders must have a leadership philosophy. As we cave in to the "me too" pressure, we frantically assemble a philosophy of our own. After days or weeks of effort, we end up with a lengthy manifesto that articulates our leadership philosophy in terms worthy of inclusion in a Ph.D. program syllabus. We eagerly forward the document to our teams and our bosses, with an excited note proclaiming our accomplishment. We think to ourselves, *Since I finally have a leadership philosophy of my own, I must be a leader in the organization now, right?*

Then it happens. Our team members open the document. They see "Page 1 of 13" and their eyes glaze over. As leaders, we have succumbed to the pressure of business schools and their frameworks. We are suckers for consultants and their buzzwords. We fawn over the latest and greatest phrases to better define who we are as leaders, only to find that those words lack emotion and conviction. Sometimes we are simply emulating leaders at levels above us who have used fancy words to define their leadership philosophy, and we choose to use fancy words too. These pressures and weaknesses on our part are turning us into vapid clones. When this happens, we are turning leadership into something disingenuous, ephemeral, and bland.

We all know what buzzwords are. We can all sniff out B.S. when we hear it. This is not a treatise written to define those terms. What I will do, though, is explain the negative effects these kinds of words can have on you and your team.

Buzzwords come in many forms. They can be used to describe new business ideas, creative concepts, or complex thoughts. Buzzwords can create a common vocabulary that serves as shorthand to cut through the complexity. They are also used to convey broad platitudes no one will disagree with. This form of buzzword is perfect for inclusion in leadership philosophies. Who doesn't want to be on a team that "maximizes value" and "leverages the full potential of our associates," anyway?

There are two major problems with including words like these in your leadership philosophy. First, those concepts are not actionable. They leave things open to broad interpretation. Your definition of "maximizing value" may differ from mine. That difference in definition could lead me to take actions you might not like, but both of us would still be right, because we are taking action according to our personal definitions of value. Second, buzzwords provide no insight whatsoever into the person speaking them. These words could come out of the mouths of a hundred different leaders. In every case, one would know nothing more about that person after hearing those words than before hearing them.

There is an old adage: *Soldiers do not fight for country. They do not fight for values. They do not fight for gods. When the shooting starts, soldiers fight for the soldier next to them in the foxhole.* This concept holds true for leaders on the corporate battlefield. Your team does not follow you and respect you because of your title. They follow and respect you because of the person you are. Buzzwords prevent your team from ever getting to know the real you. If they do not know the real you, the chances of their fighting hard alongside you in the trenches of business combat are far less than they should be.

Bullshit is even worse than buzzwords. I struggled mightily with whether or not to term it "bullshit" in a book dedicated to professional leadership. Sure, there are more genteel ways to describe bluster, bravado, and exaggeration, but I have yet to find a term that more accurately describes the stream of meaningless, disingenuous words that issue forth from the mouths of the self-aggrandizing. I could try to dance around the word with softer choices, but I would be generating my own pile of it, which I am sure you would not tolerate. If you take offense at the term, please accept my apologies. Let's simply consider the term as shorthand for all the things people say but do not really mean, or do mean but exaggerate so that others will think more highly of them. I will not belabor my explanation of why using such words at work is destructive. Suffice it to say that being a purveyor of it destroys your credibility, makes you appear boorish, and genuinely diminishes the respect people have for you as a leader. These meaningless words and phrases have a way of creeping into written versions of leadership philosophies because they sound great on paper and make us feel much more important than we really are.

The only way I know to roll back the tide of all this meaningless jargon is to say what you really mean. Words spoken from the heart and the gut are clear, concise, meaningful, and genuine. They help ground you and your team. They signal that you are willing to take a stand for something you believe in instead of watering down your beliefs with complicated words so you will not offend someone or so your simple thoughts will sound more important. You must realize that such approaches have exactly the opposite effect. Using buzzwords makes you sound less intelligent. Filling your leadership philosophy with obscure or hard-to-define concepts diminishes people's trust in you. Both behaviors are counterproductive and hinder you from reaching your goal of becoming an authentic leader. That is why you are here, isn't it?

Allow me to share a story that demonstrates both the trouble that jargon-filled leadership philosophies can cause and the way that one executive avoided such a trap. I know several executives who were members of the same senior leadership team. Following a reorganization, their new boss, Jared, worked hard to get the team to gel. After several months of effort, it simply was not happening. The team members were mistrustful both of Jared and of each other. Team meetings were painful, and one-on-one sessions with Jared were even worse. The team was quickly devolving into chaos.

Jared decided he would break through the dysfunction by getting everyone on the team to know each other better as people and as leaders. He held a three-day-long offsite where he and a consultant he knew well worked with the team members on leadership. They discussed what leadership meant to them. They related leadership to the corporate competency model. They discussed job descriptions and how they could make leadership stand out as a critical skill set.

The seminal event of the offsite required each leader to share his or her leadership philosophy with the group. The expectation was the philosophy would be a typewritten document the leader would read aloud. Jared read his leadership philosophy first. It said all the right things. It emphasized the importance of teamwork, trust, hard work, and fun. He read it passionately and thoughtfully. When he finished ten minutes later, he asked the other team members to share their leadership philosophies with the group. After the third reading, the room sounded like a beehive from all the buzzwords.

Craig, one of the team members, grew more and more visibly uncomfortable and frustrated with every reading. By the time all the other team members finished reading their leadership philosophies, Craig's lips were nothing more than a short, thin line covering his clenched teeth. He gently shook his head from side to side as he stood to take his turn. He set his typewritten leadership philosophy homework aside and took a moment to look each of his colleagues in the eye. Craig's gaze stopped at Jared. With a calm, clear voice Craig stated, "My leadership philosophy is simple: *Say what you mean. Do what you say.*" He then turned and took his seat again. With eight short words Craig had said more than every other member of the team, combined. Those two sentences enabled him to swat away the buzzwords and quickly share a clear articulation of his standards, his beliefs, and his code of conduct. Everyone on the team instantly knew what he expected of them and what they could expect of him. Craig's statement was practical and applicable to every interaction he could ever have at work. Just like that, he demonstrated the power of one well-crafted leadership maxim. As a result of Craig's actions, several members of the leadership team later shortened their own philosophies, and the members of Craig's team always knew how he felt about any situation and what he planned on doing about it.

This book debunks the conventional wisdom that leadership philosophies must be full of buzzwords. It destroys the myth that the longer the philosophy is, the better it must be. *Clear, meaningful,* and *simple* are the rules that apply to maxims. By replacing buzzwords with personal stories and experience, you will humanize yourself as a leader. In many cases you will endear yourself to your team. They will understand what you stand for and appreciate the time and effort you put into distilling your philosophy down into a short, crisp document. Throwing a bunch of words on paper is easy. Figuring out which words truly matter and arranging them in an accessible and compelling way takes energy and thought. It is that kind of energy I am asking you to invest in writing your maxims. The leadership maxims approach will help any leader articulate a leadership philosophy on one piece of paper. This approach will help you make leadership personal, inspiring, and exciting again.

PART 2

[LEADING YOURSELF]

CHAPTER 3

[LEARNING TO LEAD YOURSELF]

The first step in articulating your leadership maxims is determining how you will lead yourself. Nobody is going to follow you if you do not know where you are going. You need to have a clear set of goals and standards for yourself, because it enables you to focus on what's important and it gives your team something to identify with and support. If you don't have a clear direction or well-articulated values, your efforts can become diluted and ineffective and your team will very likely become confused about who you really are and what's important to you. By creating maxims focused on leading yourself, you can eliminate this potential lack of focus and confusion.

THE IMPORTANCE OF LEADING YOURSELF

There are two reasons we are starting this work with defining how you will lead yourself. First, a journey is defined not only by the endpoint but also by the start. For your voyage to be successful, you must have a clear understanding of where you are now, where you are going, and how you would like to reach your destination. Second, as you rise in the leadership ranks, you personally have more followers and fewer leaders. Your leaders' expectations of you get higher and higher with every rung of the ladder you climb. Gone are the days when your boss would give you detailed coaching and feedback. You are in the big leagues now, or at least you are aspiring to move up from the minor leagues soon. Although fewer people are leading you and they are giving you less and less guidance along the way, this does not mean you do not need to be led. Rather, this means you need to take ownership for your own development and growth. The days of the paternalistic organization are long gone. There are no more thirty-year careers at the same company with a nice fat pension waiting for you at the end. These days you are in charge of your career, your training, your motivation, and your advancement. If you do not step up and fill the leadership void around you, your career will stall, your team will falter, and you will be generally disappointed with your lot in life. Leading yourself is the foundation on which your future success and happiness depends.

I personally learned the importance of leading myself the hard way. As a young consultant, I was responsible for one third of our team's output because there were only three of us on the team. We were helping our client create new lines of business and pursue new growth opportunities. Despite being a reasonably seasoned professional after five years in the army and a year as a consultant, I was still pretty immature. My previous consulting project managers had taken an active role in both my client work and my career development. This project was different. My manager was tough on me. He always seemed to be asking for more, yet compared to my previous managers, he was providing less guidance, direction, and feedback. The quality of my work never seemed to be good enough. He would indicate I hadn't been rigorous in my thinking or had not pushed the client team members far enough on the creation of our deliverables. Eventually I became frustrated with the project. I began "mailing it in" and skating by on less-than-solid work. My thinking was uninspired and my deliverables were not of the highest quality. It became a painfully long four months.

The whole time I was submitting low-quality materials, I was whining about the lack of guidance and support from my manager. It seemed all I did was complain about the absence of direction and feedback. Needless to say, when I received my performance review at the end of the project, it was as uninspiring as the work I had done. Initially I was disappointed and frustrated. How could I possibly receive a "needs improvement" rating when I was not getting the leadership I believed I needed from my manager?

During the performance appraisal conversation, it hit me. My manager pointed out that I was in a role that required client leadership and thought leadership. He explained how he expected me to step up and take ownership for the quality of my own work as well as set the standards for the members of the client team. His role was leadership of the entire project, and he had counted on me to lead my part of the project with minimal guidance and intervention. The lights went on for me when he said, "If you want to take on bigger project leadership roles, you first have to demonstrate you can motivate yourself to deliver the quality of work I know you're capable of." Ouch. His comment cut to the core of the issue. I had abdicated responsibility for my own performance, growth, and development. My manager had higher expectations of me, and I had failed to meet them.

From that point forward I took a much more active role in managing my performance, setting high standards for myself, and taking responsibility for my own motivation. It was a painful lesson, but I had to learn it. After that performance review I relied much more on myself to drive my performance and future projects went much better. After the performance review I became more fully aware of my shortcomings. And although I did not consciously give it that name at the time, I created an idea of a "future me"—a person who would be fully accountable for his own work. From then on I relied much more on myself to set and achieve standards of performance.

CREATING A FUTURE YOU

Although the importance of leading yourself cannot be denied, the notion of leading yourself is an odd one if you think about this concept literally. I am actually asking you to briefly step outside of yourself *today* and look at *future* you and who you want to be. By stepping out of the moment you are in, you can construct a future vision of who you want to be and create a plan for how you can become that person. That future you is the person who will lead today's you forward to a better place.

When you first begin thinking about future you, visions of wealth, retirement, the physical location of your retirement home, and several other tangible attributes may immediately come to mind. Yes, those things are important, but that is not what we are going to focus on. All those things are outcomes resulting from the path you choose and the choices you make along your road to becoming future you. Some of those things might happen completely independently of the person you become. Future you could be the meanest person in the world, but if you hit the lottery, future you will still be rich. Future you could have the strongest character and values on Earth, but your home and all your possessions could be blown away in a hurricane. The material attributes of future you are irrelevant, because what matters is what is left when the hurricane passes or all the lottery money is spent. Who is the person standing there in the end, and what kind of human being is that person? Those are the questions you need to explore.

To successfully lead yourself, you need to find the person underneath the tangible and superficial things. As you begin defining future you, think about the character of that individual. Imagine that person's values. Consider what that person stands for and represents to those around him or her. That is the future you that we are seeking to create. But before we can describe the person you want to become, we have to understand the person you are today.

Just as I had to know and understand myself and come to terms with my own weaknesses in order to grow, you have to do the same. If you are going to successfully lead yourself, you cannot skip this step. Your background, values, and experiences to date are the raw materials you have to work with. Understanding your current beliefs, biases, blessings, and curses will help you formulate an achievable vision of future you. Yes, that vision should be aspirational, but it must also be within the realm of possibility. If it is not, you will get discouraged thinking that you can never achieve your goal, and you will be more likely to give up on the journey to reach your destination. That future vision must also be consistent with who you are now. If it is not, you will be trying to become something you are not, and everyone will eventually see you for the fraud you are. Even worse, there will come a day when you realize you have been trying to become someone you do not truly believe in. In that moment you will experience a painful and terrifying identity crisis.

If you want to grow and become someone different from who you are today, understanding yourself now and identifying the behaviors you no longer want is the only way to change them and move forward. Knowing yourself requires taking a hard look in the mirror and assessing your character, warts and all. We all have our deficiencies. True leaders are honest, sometimes painfully so, in their self-assessment. They can admit they have weaknesses, and they actively move toward strengthening them or mitigating their deleterious effects. By leading an examined life and objectively assessing yourself, you send a strong message to those around you. You are telling them you take ownership for your growth and care about self-improvement. The leadership tone you set through these actions alone is worth more than a thousand written pages of philosophy.

WHERE TO START

To begin this introspection, sit down with a notebook or a stack of blank paper. This book will ask the questions. You will provide the answers. This will be a messy process, and you will go through quite a bit of paper before you effectively distill your maxims down to a single page. Do not strive for perfection with every phrase or idea you write initially; rather, capture the thought or feeling and continue your introspection. Come back to your notes after you take some time away from them to reflect on your thoughts. Reread them and see what new ideas and memories come to mind. See if you notice any patterns in your thoughts when you look at them with a fresh set of eyes. Regardless of where your thoughts begin, they will change as you dig deeper and learn more about yourself. The important thing is to simply start the process of documenting these thoughts on paper instead of letting them rattle around chaotically in your head. It is almost impossible to gain clarity on your ideas without writing them down, and it is even more difficult to provide that clarity to your team without a written vehicle for doing so. Your team does not have the benefit of all the ideas bouncing around in your head. All they have to go on are your words. When we share ideas verbally, we tend to use too many words, and it's easy for those words to be misunderstood or forgotten. When we commit these ideas to paper, however, they tend to be concise, easily understood, and remembered long after the first reading. Also, when a written representation of the ideas exists, it can be referenced on a regular basis.

Your ability to define what you want to be in the future and to hold yourself to higher standards is the basis on which all your other maxims will build. If you are unable to inspire yourself, how can you expect to inspire your people? To determine how you are going to lead yourself, you need to explore who you are and who you want to become.

To start the introspection process, there are five questions you need to explore:

- Why do you get out of bed every day?
- How will you shape your future?
- What guidelines do you live by?
- When you fall down, how do you pick yourself back up?
- How do you hold yourself accountable?

In the rest of this part of the book you will explore each of these questions in depth. Answering them will help you crystallize what motivates you and what your personal rules of conduct are. Without an understanding of what you care about and what your personal ethics are, you are lost. If you are lost, your team is lost. Enough said. Your responses to these questions will eventually become your personal maxims for leading yourself.

CHAPTER 4

[# WHY DO YOU
GET OUT OF BED
EVERY DAY?]

Why do you get out of bed every morning? Why are you excited to go to work?

You need to think beyond the alarm clock. Get past the coffee and getting kids ready for school. Consider what is beyond the paycheck that enables you to pay your rent or mortgage. What are the deeper answers to these questions? You need to consider the core of why you do the things you do. This maxim is about your intrinsic motivation. The answers to these two questions will help you articulate a leadership maxim that defines the kind of work you want to do.

It may surprise you, but for most people the motivation to go to work every day is not the money. For most people it is about growth. It is about challenge. It is about great coworkers. Our passions fuel us, and enlightened leaders seek to achieve their full potential. Such leaders enjoy overcoming challenges, building new skills, and having as much positive impact as they can on their organizations. The task itself becomes the reward, and our own pride and satisfaction in a job well done is compensation enough for doing it. Until you can clearly articulate what you find rewarding, you will never be able to find that kind of work. You will be stuck in a dead-end job with little prospect of success. Your workday will be lacking happiness and fulfillment. The job will not lead anywhere, because when you are not excited about the work, you are even less motivated to take on more tasks.

FINDING YOUR MOTIVATION

The better you are able to align your work with what you love to do, the more successful and fulfilled you will be as you do it. At some point in your life, there will not be anyone else to excite you and motivate you about your work; you will need to find that motivation internally. This is possible only if you love what you do, and the only way to find what you truly love is through introspection. Your job is to find your passion and turn it into a leadership maxim by crafting a phrase or drawing on an image that evokes those feelings of fulfillment and satisfaction. Creating a maxim focused on what you love to do will help you choose jobs, positions, or projects consistent with your passions. It will also help you avoid roles inconsistent with your passions, thereby keeping you out of situations where you will be unhappy with the work you are asked to do.

My maxim that answers these questions is but two words:

Light bulbs

That may not mean much to you, but it means a lot to me. Light bulbs are the reason why, when I get out of bed every day, I am excited to get to my desk to start work. I am a teacher. I teach leadership, communications, strategy, and a host of other business and professional development topics I find fascinating. I cannot help but get excited when I work with energizing and smart clients discussing their most pressing issues. These activities give me a deep sense of satisfaction.

I know when I am teaching and I make a point or a connection that resonates for a participant in the class, I have had an impact on them. The indicator I look for is that look on a person's face that says *You made a light bulb go on for me. I get it now. You have helped me have a moment of clarity.* Those are the meaningful moments in my work. Turning light bulbs on for people is why I am excited to go to work every day.

More important than simply having the maxim of "light bulbs" is how I use it to guide decisions I make. When I face a choice between, say, building a training class on presentation fonts or creating a class on strategic planning skills, "light bulbs" helps guide me toward working on the one I will enjoy more. I would much rather write and teach a course on business strategy than I would on the merits of Times New Roman versus Arial Bold. I will do a better job teaching the strategy course because I know I will be turning on light bulbs for the participants. I cannot conceive of turning light bulbs on for people when I tell them Comic Sans is a terrible font for their purpose. The maxim helps guide me toward not only work I will enjoy but also work that I will do well and that will be more effective for those I am teaching. Because our lives end up being the summation of the decisions we make, having a consistent maxim I can use in my decision-making process serves to keep me focused on more satisfying and rewarding work and steers me toward a fulfilling professional career.

Light bulbs. They are two simple words that hold a great deal of meaning and serve as a perfect maxim—for me. I hope this example illustrates how to create maxims that are meaningful for you and how they can guide the choices you make. Maxims are simple, personally meaningful, and easy to explain. After reading about the importance light bulbs hold for me, you likely have no remaining questions as to my internal motivation and why I get out of bed and rush to work every day. If you were a member of my team, knowing my maxim would give you a better understanding of me as a leader. That understanding helps build trust and a productive working relationship.

One leader I knew had a song as his maxim. Tim was a jovial guy. The times he was happiest at work were those when he was making others laugh, smile, and feel good about themselves. He loved bringing levity to the workplace, regardless of the daily chaos that regularly surrounded him.

The jobs he held over the years were eclectic. He had been a project manager at a manufacturing company, a recruiter at a technology company, and a call center manager at a financial services firm. Regardless of the role, if you saw Tim interacting with people on his team, he was always working hard to bring smiles to their faces. He would make jokes, point out the lighter side of difficult situations, or remind people of the good things going on in their lives. This is not to say he spent all day clowning around and not getting his work done. He got his work done with a healthy dose of smiling thrown in.

All Tim's roles were seemingly unrelated. But if you asked him to explain what they had in common, he would start humming the tune of Scott Joplin's rag "The Entertainer" (which you may remember from the movie *The Sting*), and it was hard not to hum along. Says Tim,

> Every job I've ever had has always given me the opportunity to make other people smile. I'm a colorful guy. I enjoy being on stage and performing for others. I like making their troubles go away by reminding them it's okay to have fun. I've found I gravitate toward roles where I interact with people all day long and where the jobs can be either pressure-filled or frustrating. I've always seen a big part of my job as being the person who entertains people, makes them smile, and gets them to temporarily forget their troubles. I've always been the entertainer. That's what I do and that's who I am. I enjoy that aspect of my work more than any other.

That song was Tim's maxim. As he considered every job opportunity placed before him, the important evaluation criteria were whether or not he would regularly work with people as opposed to being an individual contributor and whether the company's culture would support him in being uniquely himself. He chose roles that gave him the freedom to lead in his own special way, in which his lighthearted nature would be valued and appreciated.

While Tim was working at the call center, management changed. His new boss was exceedingly focused on metrics and had little tolerance for what he termed "goofing around." Tim tried to adapt to the new boss's style, but he found himself unhappy on his drive home every night. He felt like the volume of his song was being slowly dialed down to zero. Ultimately Tim left that job and pursued his longtime dream of teaching and playing guitar. He found deep satisfaction in giving the gift of music to others who were eager to learn. Tim was always thrilled to take the stage on occasion and perform for others because he saw how his music took the audience away from their troubles, even if only for a moment.

"The Entertainer" was Tim's reminder of what he was about and what his passions were. His maxim was a tune from 1902. My maxim is two words that, when written on a piece of paper, will likely have no resonance for anyone other than me. The point is, it does not matter what you choose as your maxim, as long as it has a deep personal resonance.

WRITING YOUR MAXIMS

Now it is your turn to write a maxim.

For you to document your leadership philosophy on one piece of paper, you must go through the exercise of writing things down. Start by thinking about accomplishments you are proudest of or activities you derive great satisfaction from. Answer the following questions and write down the first things that come to mind:

- Why do you get out of bed every morning?
- Why are you excited to go to work?
- When people ask you what you love to do, what is your response?
- What do you tell people you are really great at doing?

All of these questions are designed to get at what really motivates you. If you are having trouble with these questions, try filling in the blank in this sentence to get to the heart of what makes you tick: "I am driven by a need to _____." It might be that easy. If it's not, reach deep into your memories to find the times you were most excited about your work. This first set of questions is designed to generate the raw material of powerful memories on which your maxim will be based.

Once you've settled on a few memories, try answering these questions about them:

- What were the circumstances surrounding those times?
- What was it about the activity or activities that excited you? Was it the challenge? Was it the learning? Was it simply the act of doing?
- Why did you enjoy that work so much?

As the answers come to you, write them down. You do not need a long narrative. Simply write down the words, phrases, or images that come to mind as you consider these questions.

This is not an easy process. Be honest in your answers and don't rush yourself. You are trying to create something authentic and intensely personal. Once you do have your thoughts written down and are happy with the results, think about specific and personal reminders of those times when your work excited you. It can be a phrase, a comment someone made, a song that reminds you of that period, the name of someone who was there and meaningfully involved in the event, or anything else that jogs your memory and takes you back to that time. For example, if you are passionate about helping people grow and take on new roles and you helped someone get promoted, your maxim might be something like "Susan's promotion ceremony." You need to tie your passion back to an event or a concept that has strong emotional meaning for you. Write down that reminder as simply and directly as you can. *Do not include buzzwords.* The only things you should include are the words that cut to the essence of that concept.

Got it? Congratulations! That is your first leadership maxim.

Remember my maxim? Light bulbs. Light bulbs are why I get out of bed in the morning and why I'm excited to go to the office. When people ask me what I love to do, I tell them I love teaching new ideas and watching as my students come to that sudden moment of understanding. And yes, I'm good at it. The times I'm most excited about my work are when I'm creating those "Aha!" moments for people. Look again at the first list of questions: "light bulbs" answers all of them for me.

You are probably looking at your first maxim and wondering if it is any good. After all, it is only a short phrase or sentence. Does it answer the questions for you as mine does for me? To test its strength, ask yourself the following additional questions. If your maxim is going to positively alter and guide your behavior, it must be strong.

- Does the maxim quickly remind me of something I find important and meaningful?
- Do I feel strong emotions (either positive or negative) when I read the maxim and remember the story behind it?
- If someone asks me what the maxim means, can I easily explain it and tell the story behind it in such a way that they understand me better as a person?
- When I share the story with others, am I sharing something deeply personal or sharing something superficial?
- Will the story behind the maxim remind me how I would like to behave—or not behave—in similar or applicable situations?
- If I regularly make decisions consistent with this maxim's intent, will I be doing things that excite and inspire me?

If you answered "yes" to all these questions, you have created a good maxim. If any of your answers were "no," go back and dig deeper into what excites you and ensure that the maxim you create enables you to answer these questions in the affirmative. When you have finished, write the maxim down in Appendix B of this book. If you are satisfied with what you have written—and, ideally, excited by it—you can consider the maxim done. If you are not quite happy with it, leave it alone for now and come back to it later. You may find that creating more maxims in the following pages will help you clarify this one related to your source of inspiration. If you are stuck on this one, set it aside, keep reading and creating your maxims, and then return to it. Your continued reflection and introspection should help you unlock your true motivation and enable you to answer the question of why you go to work every day.

It is important to understand what motivates and inspires you. The understanding of your internal motivation will help you pursue activities consistent with what excites you. When you work toward a focused goal, you will likely find yourself working harder and persevering through difficult times because you are excited about both the work itself and the rewards attached to it. It is much easier to get out of bed every day when you are eager to begin working on things you find interesting and fulfilling.

CHAPTER 5

[HOW WILL YOU SHAPE YOUR FUTURE?]

When was the last time you paused and really thought about your future? Who is future you? Where are you headed with your life? What will your end game look like? What will be the summation of all the actions you take during the course of your life? This is not an exploration of your stock portfolio or retirement plan; it is about stepping back from your day-to-day life and asking yourself where you want to end up and what sort of person you want to be.

By articulating what you want to be and what you stand for as a person, you can convey a great deal about your values, goals, aspirations, and dreams to members of your team and your coworkers. Once they understand these aspects of you, your actions will make more sense to them. The decisions you make will take on deeper meaning because they will understand your goals and have the context from which you are making those choices. They will know you better as a person, which will help them trust you more as a leader.

DEFINING YOUR FUTURE

If you paint a compelling enough picture of your future, it will be easy to make choices consistent with that desired future state. The self-reinforcing nature of that dynamic continuously improves the likelihood that you will arrive at your preferred destination. You will make choices you are happy with. Those choices will open new possibilities for you. Many of those possibilities will be exciting and fulfilling. You will likely choose the most fulfilling ones, and the cycle will renew itself.

For me, the future is all about learning and teaching. It is a virtuous circle: a positive cycle in which one positive event leads to another, which in turn leads to one beyond that. Learning new ideas or disciplines fascinates me. Interconnecting those experiences and disciplines and creating new ideas to share with others through teaching is even more exciting. And the more I teach, the more I learn from my class participants, and that learning renews the virtuous circle. My finest professional moments (and even many personal ones) occur when I am teaching someone something new. When I see light bulbs go on for people, I feel a deep sense of fulfillment. Even better are the times when I see connections I have made and insights I have had become new knowledge I am able to share with others. The entire process of learning, sharing, and growing is the most professionally fulfilling work I have ever done; I want to continue doing it well into the future. When I add those concepts and feelings together, I arrive at this maxim:

He never stopped learning, teaching, and coaching.

This is who I want the future me to be—someone who is always learning, teaching, and coaching. When people remember me and talk about me when I am gone, I want that conversation to be about all the things they learned from me. I want them to remember how I took every opportunity afforded to me to learn, teach, and coach. I want to be remembered for helping people to grow and be more than they ever thought they could be.

Notice how this maxim is consistent with my light bulbs maxim. Light bulbs remind me why I go to work every day. They help me see the positive impact I have on people and reinforce my behaviors to be consistent with achieving those results. Light bulbs are about my present reality.

This learning, teaching, and coaching maxim takes light bulbs one step further. It makes me aspire to a future in which I am not only turning on the light bulbs but also generating the insights and knowledge that cause those light bulbs to go on. Those insights are created through ongoing learning on my part. This maxim is aspirational. Is it certain I will always turn on a light bulb for every class participant? Not by a long shot. Is it highly probable that if I focus on that aspiration I will take actions consistent with achieving it? Definitely.

This is a deeply personal maxim. It gives insight into what makes me tick. I am building my relationship with those I share it with because I am sharing my dream and helping them understand me as a person. The maxim sets a clear direction—for me. It helps me make decisions. When I am faced with a choice of doing A or doing B, this maxim helps me select the option most consistent with who I am trying to become as a person. As I apply this maxim to situations I encounter, it helps me choose the more satisfying roles, jobs, and tasks aligned with the destination I am trying to get to. This is not to say this maxim always applies to every choice I make. But when it does apply, it helps me build internal consistency between who I want to be and the actions I take to become that person.

I'm human. There are times I do not live up to the goal of always learning or always teaching. When I fail to meet my standard, I feel a profound sense of disappointment. My learning, teaching, and coaching maxim stares me in the face and enables me to judge my own performance. When my performance falls short, the maxim serves as a reminder of the standard I have set for myself and what I need to do to achieve it. It helps me refocus on my goal and be mindful of the choices I make. The maxim also points out my failures and how they affect the likelihood of my arriving at my chosen destination.

Here is an example of how this maxim has guided my behavior. As an entrepreneur I do not have a boss telling me what to do. Sure, my clients ask things of me, but as far as the day-to-day running of my business, many decisions are up to me. When I first started my current business, I did not have coworkers and was essentially on my own as far as how the business ran. Of course I sought input from trusted advisors, but in the end it always came down to a choice I had to make.

As I tried to grow the business, opportunities for new sources of revenue presented themselves. Some were basic consulting projects that would have paid well but did not require the creation of new knowledge nor was there much teaching involved in them. Other opportunities centered around training in some basic skill sets, like how to build spreadsheet models or create pretty PowerPoint slides. Yes, there was teaching involved in those, but not much in the way of insight or new knowledge generation and conveyance. I faced a dilemma: doing unfulfilling work in exchange for cash, or walking away from the cash and focusing on work more consistent with learning, teaching, and coaching. Do you have any idea how hard it is to walk away from cash when you are starting a business? It is almost impossible. It is so hard to do that I didn't. I took on a consulting project that lacked a focus on learning, teaching, and coaching. The work centered on an industry in which I had expertise, but it was also one I had left a long time ago. The project was blocking and tackling strategic planning and business development. Little of it was about client skill building or knowledge creation. It was completely inconsistent with the kind of work I had proclaimed I wanted to do.

But of course there was a twist. The consulting work took up only 70 percent of my time. I focused the other 30 percent on building my training and coaching services, which I considered to be my core business. I looked at the consulting as a means to an end. It was a part-time job (albeit a big part of my time) that helped me reach a more important goal. I never considered the consulting project a core part of my company's service offerings. It was simply a way to maintain cash flow for my business while I worked hard to grow the true focus of my firm—the training and coaching. After a year at my part-time job, the consulting engagement came to an end. By that time, the training business had taken off and I was able to transition to focusing on it full-time.

My light bulbs maxim and my learning, teaching, and coaching maxim helped me stay true to what I want to do long-term. Those maxims helped me keep the consulting work in perspective. They reminded me daily that the consulting work was a part-time job and that I also had to expend significant energy building the training side of my business. The maxims prevented the consulting and the associated cash from taking over and crushing my real aspirations to teach and coach. It is true that the maxims did not keep me entirely from doing work inconsistent with where I wanted to go. They did, however, help me maintain focus on what was important and steer me away from work that was not aligned with my goals as soon as practically possible. Maxims are not always black and white. They are sometimes gray, but they help you see the light side and the dark side of decisions you have to make.

Since that consulting project, I have had similar opportunities cross my desk. Many of them have been standard consulting work or have centered on technical skills training. Neither of those types of work helps me turn on light bulbs over people's heads. Neither is consistent with my always learning, teaching, and coaching. I now routinely say "no" to those projects. Yes, it can be painful, because it involves walking away from significant amounts of cash. But saying "no" prevents me from working on things that do not excite me. The time and energy I save by not doing those projects are dedicated to building the part of my business I love—training and coaching. The more training work I do, the happier I am and the more passionate I become about the business. The virtuous circle ensues where passion becomes performance. Performance becomes repeat business. Repeat business funds the passion, and good things continue to happen. These two maxims help me keep the virtuous circle humming along, undisturbed by distracting projects along the way. The more that circle spins, the higher my chances of achieving my aspiration of future me being a guy who always learns, teaches, and coaches.

WRITING YOUR MAXIMS

When answering the questions that will help you create your own maxim, you need to set aside all expectations others might have of you and arrive at your own conclusions. Do not be swayed by opinions of others and their beliefs of what you "ought to be" striving for, but instead seek your own answers. These questions require true focus and dedicated time alone, so I suggest you explore them away from distractions. Allot a substantial amount of time for this thinking. Perhaps go take a long walk in the park or along the shore of your favorite body of water to help get out of your daily grind and clear your head. You need some uninterrupted "me time" to come to your answers for this maxim.

As you are considering this future vision of who you want to become and where you want to go, unburden yourself of reality. Step out of the moment you are in now and place yourself in a time as far into the future as you can imagine. The moment you are in right now means nothing. Yes, being in the moment is a critical part of being fulfilled and not missing life as it passes by, but it is equally important to have direction in your own life before you can impart direction to the lives of others. To find that direction, stepping out of the current moment is critical. Your personal situation can constrain the way you think about the future. Your present job, financial picture, family, friends, skills, and opinions all can cloud your view of what is possible. The only way to see as far ahead as you need to is to remove those clouds from your view. Don't worry—we will come back to your present reality soon enough. Enjoy the break from it while we figure out exactly where you are headed.

To create this maxim, you must set aside not only present-day constraints but future externalities as well. You cannot control the future. Stock market crashes, wars, mergers, layoffs, and myriad other events that will make an impact on your life are completely out of your control. All you can control is the way you show up in an unpredictable world. If you define your future destination based on the way you expect the world's events to unfold, you are not leading—you are contingency planning. Leaders lay out a desired future state, then mold the world around them to make it happen. Can you truly bend every aspect of the future to your will? No. Regardless of the future state you lay out and no matter how great a leader you are, you cannot prevent many of those future events from happening. What you can do, however, is define the character of the person standing in the midst of that chaos. The definition of that person means the will you must bend is your own. You must overcome the inertia of who you are today and create momentum toward who you want to be tomorrow.

Now for the tricky bit—the introspection. How do you define your future self? Focus on yourself and the person you want to become regardless of what happens in the world around you. This is about defining you first and then how you will react to the world. This reverses our normal way of thinking, whereby we first define the potential future world and then adapt to that external environment. To make this mental shift, you need but answer two powerful questions:

- What do I want my epitaph to say?
- What do I want the summation of my career (or more loftily, my life) to be?

These are difficult questions to ask, and the answers are hard to imagine. I never said this was going to be an easy or comfortable process. Remember, though, when answering these questions, to remove any current concerns about your job, your net worth, and your title and to block out any future worldly events that might affect you. These questions focus exclusively on you and what you stand for as a person. They are designed to cut through all the extraneous events and expectations surrounding you and expose the true core of your aspirations in life. If, for example, your lifetime goal is to be a prolific author because you have a message you want to share with the world, your maxim might be something like "*New York Times* #1 bestseller." Choose a maxim that inspires you to reach for goals that are personally meaningful to you in terms of how they define who you want to become.

You already know my maxim: "He was always learning, teaching, and coaching." I would be happy for this to be my epitaph. What about you?

If nothing comes to mind right away, try again to free yourself of your present situation. Think beyond your current job description or career path. This should be an exercise of removing limitations. You need to think in terms of your legacy. Fill in the blanks in this sentence: "(Your name) stood for (blank) and we'll never forget (blank) about him/her." Write down the first things that come to mind. Remember— no buzzwords. No artificial views of what you think others want you to be. This is about the real you.

Once you have collected some thoughts on what you stand for and what you want people to remember about you, think about something you identify with those qualities. Here are some questions to get you started:

- Are there any experiences you have had in which you exhibited those desired characteristics?
- Is there someone in your life who personifies these ideals?
- Is there a book, song, movie, or poem that reminds you of these aspirations?

To write this maxim, you are looking for a simple reminder of what these ideals are. Write down the ideas that resonate most deeply for you. Come back to those ideas in a few days and reread them. Remember—the maxims process is one of reflection and introspection. Taking a break from your work enables you to turn the ideas over in your head a few times during that time away. When you come back to your work, you might look at it through a new lens, and new ideas might coalesce. Once you have taken some time away, review what you've written and then choose the story, phrase, or concept that resonates most powerfully for you. Identify something about that memory or story that will help you quickly recall it and remember what about it inspires you. Choose the simplest statement or reminder you can that quickly encapsulates who you want future you to be. Write that concept down—it is the first draft of your maxim.

As you review this maxim, you need to ensure that it is strong enough to guide your behavior. To test its strength, ask yourself the following questions:

- Can I see myself using this maxim to guide future career decisions?
- Can I easily explain the story behind the maxim, such that people will clearly understand where I am trying to go with my life?
- When I read this maxim, do I immediately think "Yeah! That's what I'm all about!"?

If you answered "yes" to these questions, you have created a solid maxim for defining future you. Document it on the maxims worksheet in Appendix B.

Defining future you is a critical step in the leadership maxims creation process. It provides direction and context to your everyday decisions. This maxim will help you to stay focused on your life goals and to make choices consistent with achieving them. When you eventually share this maxim with members of your team, they will get a clear sense for what motivates and excites you, which will give them a better perspective of who you are as an individual. That understanding helps build the trust all people need to have in their leaders.

CHAPTER 6

[WHAT GUIDELINES DO YOU LIVE BY?]

In your last maxim you defined a goal for yourself. Goals are great for setting direction, but how do you keep yourself on course? In a world full of mounting pressures and global competition, it is harder and harder to get ahead and easy to lose perspective. Throw in a large dose of ambition and drive, plus a touch of insecurity, and you have the potential for unhealthy things to happen. Our judgment can get warped. We can make decisions under pressure we will not be happy with when the pressure is off. Perhaps we will find we have turned into that tyrant boss we always hated. Or we have become the absent parent we vowed we would never become. We might learn, much to our chagrin, that we are viewed as the backstabbing coworker who will do anything to get ahead. Our drive and ambition to get to our destination can turn us into the kind of person we would never want to be, or at the least tempt us to take actions inconsistent with being the leaders we aspire to be.

WHY WE NEED GUIDELINES

We all need guidance during challenging times. We need something to keep us within healthy and productive boundaries. We are human and make mistakes. Having personal guidelines that we live our lives by will remind us how we want to behave; it helps keep us safe and on track. This does not have to be a detailed list of do's and don'ts. A laundry list of rules and regulations is not practical. Instead, a judgment-based approach that can be broadly applied to any situation is much more flexible, manageable, and applicable. Every situation is different, and each decision we face will involve a variety of new and unpredictable factors. But if we have judgment-based guidelines to govern our conduct, we can apply them to any situation we face instead of having to frantically search a list of do's and don'ts only to find that particular situation is not covered. The simpler the guidelines, the more powerful they can be.

When you write this maxim, you will create simple, judgment-based guidelines. You need to construct your guidelines during calm times. The more thoughtful you can be when you write these maxims, the stronger and more broadly applicable they can be when you need to use them. Writing them during a period when you face few pressures will prevent you from succumbing to the temptation to craft them in ways that leave loopholes to excuse current behavioral shortcomings. For example, imagine you are on a deadline-driven project that requires you to cut some ethical corners to finish on time. If you write your maxim during that stress-filled period, you could end up constructing it in such a way that those small ethical lapses are permissible as long as there are no big ethical "prison-worthy" breaches. If, however, you wrote the maxim before that project, those small ethical transgressions would not be within the boundaries of acceptability and your maxim could help you avoid making those mistakes. Writing these maxims during the calm means that when the inevitable storm arrives, you will be able to rely on them knowing they are intended to help you reach your destination with your integrity safely intact.

I have been in my share of uncomfortable situations in which all the choices before me were painful ones. As much as I would have liked to have punted on the decision, I was the leader and I had to make the choice. Those uncomfortable moments were and continue to be perfect times to rely on my maxims to assist me with my decision making. Over

the years I have learned to rely on two similar maxims for these pur-
poses. They are:

What would Nana say? (Nana was my grandmother.)

It's hard to shave if you can't look yourself in the mirror.

Both maxims are straightforward and simple. Both evoke strong
emotions for me. Whose nana wouldn't stir emotions in their heart?
These maxims enable me to step outside myself and ask what another
person would think about my behavior. It is one thing to disappoint
myself. It is another thing entirely to disappoint Nana. The thought
of letting her down and doing something of which she would
disapprove is a powerful deterrent to bad behavior for me. The
shaving maxim reminds me I have to live with every decision I
make. I have to look myself in the eye every morning and be okay with
who I am.

These maxims are easy to explain and understand. They are much
harder to put into practice, especially in high-pressure situations. Permit
me to share some examples.

When I was a young platoon leader, we routinely went on field
exercises. When we returned from the field we would conduct an inventory of all our equipment. Upon returning to the motor pool after one
field exercise, my inventory revealed we had lost a tool that operated
the main gun on my tank. I thought *No big deal. I'll ask the supply
sergeant to order a new one.* When I went to him to place the order, he
informed me that particular tool cost $2,600 to replace. That was 10
percent of my annual salary! Even worse, such a large financial loss
would require a formal investigation into the circumstances surrounding the loss and could result in disciplinary action. This was not exactly
the way I had planned on starting my military career. I frantically
went to my platoon sergeant, who was my second-in-command, for
assistance.

He said, "Don't worry sir. Come see me after lunch." Despite his assurances, I worried.

When I saw him after lunch he said, "Go to the store and buy two Coleman propane camping stoves, and I'll have the tool in your hands by the end of the day. One of the guys in our sister battalion has an extra one but he wants a couple of field stoves for it." I felt a mix of shock and relief. On the one hand I was being extorted for two stoves to get an extra tool from a guy in a sister unit. He had likely found that tool when someone else lost it on a field exercise. For all I knew it could have even been my lost tool, as that unit had been out on the same field exercise. On the other hand, spending $80 on a couple of Coleman stoves to avoid a $2,600 wallop to my paycheck and a formal investigation seemed like a great deal.

I bought the stoves.

On reflection, I have to admit that my Nana would not have been too proud of me in making that decision. She would have told me to report the tool as lost and to find a way to resolve the problem within the unit's regulations. Had I pursued that course of action, I might have seen other possible solutions—like sending a search party down range to find the item, having all units conduct inventories to see whether we had extras that had been found previously, or taking my lumps (both financial and disciplinary) like a man.

Instead, I chose the easier path of buying my way out of a jam. In that stressful moment I did not see the real costs of my decision. By choosing that path and ignoring what Nana would have told me to do, I reinforced a culture in which barter and white-lie extortion were acceptable behaviors. As an officer partaking in this gray market economy, I was implicitly telling my soldiers it was okay for them to stock up on tools to "sell" for personal gain when someone else was in need of those items. Taking that logic one step further, I could have been encouraging soldiers to steal tools from other units to create increased demand for those items and command higher prices for them. If I had chosen to take my lumps, I might have learned better ways to resolve the situation. I definitely would have strengthened rather than weakened the moral culture of my unit. I still regret my decision. The only redeeming aspect of that choice is it regularly reinforces my belief in the strength of my maxims to help me make the right decisions regardless of the circumstances surrounding them.

Contrast the last story with the impact of my decision in the following scenario, in which I *did* follow my maxim. I had a client sign a contract for training services with my firm. Our verbal agreement called for a specific price per participant in the class and guaranteed a minimum number of participants. When I received the written contract, I noticed the client's procurement team had made an error in the wording of the pricing section. The way they had worded it would have led to them paying me substantially more than the verbal agreement called for. I asked myself *What would Nana say?* The answer was immediately clear.

I emailed the client and let her know there was an error in the pricing section of the contract. I sent her a corrected version of the contract and explained how the way it was originally worded would have resulted in them paying me several thousand dollars more than we had verbally agreed on.

Her response was one of disbelief. "Wait . . . you're telling me we made an error in our contract and we would pay you more than we originally agreed? And you are voluntarily pointing this out so we pay you less?" Needless to say, the story about my proactively making this correction rapidly made its way around the client's organization. My firm's already-excellent reputation with the client was enhanced substantially after this interchange. The long-term value of doing what Nana would say was the right choice was far greater than the short-term benefit I would have achieved had I let the error slip by without mentioning it. Furthermore, if I had let that error pass and it was later noticed by the client, it could have earned me a reputation for being at best sloppy in my contracting, and at worst selfish and deceptive. Granted, it was not a stressful time when I made this decision, but imagine if my firm had been having financial difficulties when this occurred. It would have been much harder to follow Nana's advice, yet her guidance still would have been sound. Good maxims help you make good decisions and keep you on your chosen path. Although good ethics do not always lead to good business outcomes, good ethics maxims are important to have if you want good life outcomes.

My two maxims about Nana and looking in the mirror help me make good ethical choices. I am not willing to take actions that would disappoint Nana or that would make it hard for me to look at myself in the mirror. Granted, I do not always live up to those standards, and I occasionally make poor choices. That said, I am not willing to sacrifice my ethics to achieve my personal, financial, and professional goals. I could have easily taken the payment I was not entitled to, and that extra money would have put me that much closer to my retirement goal, but doing so would have compromised my maxims. These two maxims are simple reminders of how I want to behave, and they provide direction in times when I have to make difficult choices. They are nonnegotiable for me, and I do the best I can to live up to them every day.

Javier, an executive at a manufacturing company, created this guidelines maxim: "The kids are on Facebook too." He related a story about how he had gone to a friend's holiday party and there were many photos taken of him in some funny but somewhat inappropriate poses. He had a great time at the party but received a surprise a couple of days later when his two teenage daughters began commenting on those photos of him after his friend posted them to Facebook.

> I was mortified. My girls saw photos of me that were pretty embarrassing, and even worse, they were commenting on the photos, so a bunch of their friends and our family members also saw the pictures. Even though the photos weren't scandalous, I was still uncomfortable that the girls saw them. It was a powerful reminder that everything I do might make it back to my girls—especially in an age of instant electronic communication. Now anytime I'm in a position that could be compromising, I remind myself of the Facebook photo incident, which makes me ask myself what my daughters would think if

they saw me take a specific action. If I would be embarrassed for them to learn I did something then I simply don't do it.

Javier used the photo-viewing incident to create a personal behavior guideline maxim that has deep emotional meaning for him.

WRITING YOUR MAXIMS

Let's move on to creating your maxims. Because you are still defining how you will lead yourself, these questions, like the preceding ones, call for deep introspection. I invite you to ask yourself two direct questions to define your ethical guidelines:

- What are you willing to sacrifice to reach your goals?
- What are your nonnegotiables?

Those are big, weighty questions. The answers must encompass all aspects of your life, not only what you do at work. The tradeoffs you make at work are important, but by broadening the view of where this maxim applies, you can build consistency into your behaviors in multiple arenas. Consistency will strengthen those "good behavior" muscles you are trying to better develop. It will also help you avoid a career-destroying moment that can happen when you have one set of ethical boundaries at work yet behave in a manner inconsistent with those ideals during your personal time away from work. There have been plenty of politicians and executives who have thrown their careers away not because of their work ethics, but because of their lapses in private life. If your maxim guides your behaviors both at work and at play, you reduce the risk that mistakes you make in one arena will cause difficulties in the other. It is hard to be a credible leader when your "off field" behavior directly contradicts the standards you set for yourself and your team at work.

Because these two questions are quite large, breaking them up into bite-sized chunks can help you arrive at the big answers. Here are some smaller questions to kick-start your introspection. Although you may end up with an answer to one of them becoming a maxim, the purpose is more to look for patterns in your answers to help formulate larger and broader guidelines.

- How much personal time are you willing to give up to pursue your career goals?
- How much earning potential are you willing to sacrifice to get more personal time?
- If you had to choose between a family event and an important work event, which would you choose, and how would you make that decision?
- How much of your social life is on the table for negotiation?
- What is your integrity worth to you?
- Are you willing to tell a small lie to get ahead? How about a big one? How do you differentiate between "small" and "big" lies?
- How will you choose between the harder right and the easier wrong?
- What best describes how you differentiate between the ethical and the unethical?

You must answer these questions honestly. As you read them, jot down your initial unfiltered thoughts and reactions. The answers to these questions are for you alone to see. Avoid giving what you perceive to be the *right* answer; instead, answer honestly with *your* answer. Failure to do so will lead you to create ineffective guidelines that will not keep you on track. If you do not believe your answers to these questions down to the core of your being, those answers will have no power over you when it comes time for you to make a difficult decision. Only when your answer is something you deeply believe in can you create an effective maxim from it. You can't fool yourself.

Once you have considered and answered these questions, take a step back from that paper and ask yourself *what does all this mean?* The answers to the following further questions will help you define your maxim:

- What themes are noticeable across your answers?
- Do your answers remind you of stories or situations in which you have had to make a difficult choice?

- If you made the "right" choice, what in particular about that choice would remind you to make other good choices in the future?
- If you chose poorly, how can you prevent yourself from going down that path again?

Try to distill these answers down to one or two emotionally compelling memories, phrases, stories, or images to serve as your reminder of which path to choose when you are faced with difficult options. Let these be the first draft of your maxims.

My distillation of these answers led me to my Nana maxim and my mirror maxim. Those two maxims apply in both ethical situations and situations related to nonnegotiables. For example, I know what Nana would say if I chose to work ninety hours per week, completely ignoring my family in the process. I also know what she would say about lying or choosing an easier wrong over a harder right. In writing your maxim, you are trying to achieve the same level of emotionally powerful simplicity. For example, if when you were growing up you were a member of the Boy Scouts, and your participation in scouting is a source of great pride, your maxim might be "The Scout Oath," which includes concepts of honor and morals. Focus your efforts on writing a maxim that will clearly establish a guideline you can use to differentiate right from wrong, especially in stressful situations.

To test the strength of your maxims, think back to a time when you had to make a difficult decision. That event can be a time when you made either a good or a bad choice. Now think about your newly written maxims and ask yourself these questions:

- If I had had these maxims in place at the time of that decision, would they have helped me make the right choice?
- If in that past situation I made the right choice, would I make the same choice under the guidance of these maxims?
- If I made the wrong choice back then, would these maxims have led me to make a different and better decision?

Try this back-testing approach for each maxim on several scenarios. If the maxim would guide you to the right decision in all those situations, then it is highly likely it will lead you to the right choices in the future. If the draft maxims do not lead you to the right decision all the time, ask yourself why that is the case. Modify your maxims as necessary so you can reliably count on them to safely guide you to your ultimate destination. Write the refined maxims down in Appendix B.

Maxims focused on defining and explaining your behavioral guidelines help you make better choices. These maxims define your personal code of conduct, so when you are faced with a difficult choice they will steer you toward the one most consistent with how you want to live your life. They will keep you out of trouble, and they will help your team understand how you think about the tough choices you will invariably have to make as a leader.

CHAPTER 7

[
WHEN YOU FALL DOWN, HOW DO YOU PICK YOURSELF BACK UP?
]

The maxims you have written so far will set you in the right direction. The key to moving forward, however, is understanding how you will react to and overcome the obstacles you will inevitably encounter on your journey. Maxims designed to inspire and motivate you to continue moving forward in the face of adversity increase the likelihood that you will persevere instead of giving up. There will not always be someone there to cheer you on or help you change your negative outlook about a situation. A maxim or two written during good times can serve as your inspiration during difficult ones. If written well, the maxim you create in this chapter will be your light of hope in those dark periods.

OVERCOMING YOUR OBSTACLES

Our increasingly global economy becomes more complex and unpredictable every day. The competition has gotten tougher. The paternalistic corporate mindset is long gone. There are no more guarantees of long successful careers culminating in cushy retirements. These days, everyone seems to be fighting over the same pieces of the pie. If you are fortunate enough to be designated as a "high potential" employee, you might find yourself side by side with people with sharp elbows. After all, there are not enough corner offices to go around for all of you. In this highly competitive environment, some people take the approach of making sure they shine without worrying about how others perform. They let their performance speak for itself. Others, however, focus more on bringing down their rivals than they do on boosting their own performance. You might find that you are one of those unfortunate rivals who has become a target. Or you might have a boss who, when things go wrong, protects his own advancement by throwing members of his team (like you) under the bus. Some bosses would rather blame a member of their team for a project's failure than suffer potential financial and career penalties if they take responsibility for the shortcoming. All of these are difficult situations, and you can probably name hundreds more that could fill another entire book. The bottom line is we all are going to be knocked down at some point in our lives. Sometimes we are punched, tripped, kicked in the teeth, and spat on. It is a rough-and-tumble world out there. What can you do to survive when you find yourself in such a difficult environment?

Growing up, we had our parents to pick us up, dust us off, and kiss our boo-boos when bad things happened to us. In school, we had teachers and coaches to help us when we faltered or when a bully beat us up. When we were junior employees, our bosses often came to the rescue by taking responsibility for the team's failures. All these people gave us the pep talks and told us "Get back out there and give it all you've got, kid!" when things got difficult. They sheltered and protected us from the bad things happening all around us. They provided perspective and showed us the silver lining in the storm clouds over our heads. We felt better about our world and our ability to thrive in it after we heard these motivational words from people we respected.

For many of us, those people are gone or their ability to make the clouds go away has diminished as the problems we face grow increasingly complex. Now *we* are the bosses. We do not always have someone there to help us get back on our feet. Our leaders expect us to be self-motivated and to fight our own battles. We are the ones who must help ourselves recover from setbacks—and boy, that is not always easy.

During dark times there is something even more important than motivating yourself. You must realize your team is also looking to you for cues on how to deal with bad situations. Everyone knows it when you have been knocked down. They see the project go off the rails or watch you get passed over for a promotion (or worse, receive a demotion). Your friends and colleagues (who might be future members of your team) hear about your getting laid off. They all watch carefully to see how you deal with the situation. If you sink deep into the muck of "woe is me," that attitude will be contagious. If instead you rise up and get back in the game, they will respond to that signal too. More important, you will move through the unfavorable situation and into a more productive, healthier, forward-looking place.

The first thing you must do as a leader in a difficult situation is to acknowledge how painful that predicament is. In an argument with reality you will usually lose. Expending energy wishing things were different or finding someone to blame for your problem is a waste of your precious time and energy. Take a deep breath and establish the facts of the situation. Opinions and interpretations of how a crisis came about or who is to blame for it will cloud your judgment and limit your options for action. Dedicate your energy and focus to defining your current reality, accepting it for what it is, and resolving to move forward. It is critical for you to reorient your focus away from the past event and toward positive action.

A good leadership maxim will be your tool for refocusing yourself. I have found and relied on two maxims to help me during difficult times. One helps me reframe the situation so I can tackle it more professionally and productively. The second helps me pick myself back up after I have been battered and bloodied. The following are the stories behind those maxims and how they have helped me during those dark hours.

I have been known to do my fair share of complaining. I can pout and gnash my teeth over my situation with the best of them. At one point, during a prolonged whining session led by me, a great boss of mine gave an exasperated sigh and said,

It is what it is. What are you going to do about it?

Talk about getting a well-deserved punch in the leadership nose! With but one statement and one question, he elegantly pointed out that the past had passed and my job was to lead my team forward. When I returned to my desk I added his comments to my leadership maxims. I said earlier that you should freely borrow great thoughts, sayings, and ideas from others and make them maxims of your own, providing they resonate for you personally. Since hearing him say "It is what it is" the first time, I have said that maxim to myself more times than I care to count. I have also used that maxim with members of my team, peers, bosses, and friends to help reorient the conversation in a productive direction. I used the maxim frequently with one member of my team. He knew that as soon as he came in my office to complain, I was going to turn around and point to it on the list of maxims pinned on my wall. When he would see me begin to turn, he would throw his hands in the air, say "I know. I know. What am I going to do about it?" and then promptly leave to go resolve the issue he had come to complain about. This maxim helps me admit I have fallen down and the task ahead is to stand up and get back in the fight. The maxim does the same for members of my team.

The more I have used this maxim over time, the more natural a part of how I view the world it has become. In many instances it is my first reaction to unpleasant events. It helps get me through bad situations much more rapidly than I ever believed possible. Remember the bad progress review I received after my consulting project? When the review was delivered to me, my reviewers were nervous about how I might react. Imagine their surprise when I finished reading it, set it down, and said, "It is what it is. What do we do about it?" They were dumbfounded. I made no excuses for the poor performance—the facts clearly bore out that I had been given the rating I deserved. Instead, I accepted the reality of the situation, and my maxim helped me focus on the path forward. The rest of our progress review conversation was highly productive, as we laid out a plan to create opportunities for me to demonstrate improved performance. My reviewer and I agreed on measurable milestones, and both of us committed to taking actions to help me be successful going forward. Had I not had that maxim in place, the conversation likely would have gone in a different and painful direction.

The progress review was a difficult conversation, but it was not a catastrophe. The "is what it is" maxim was sufficient for reorienting my view of the situation and making the discussion productive. But what about times when I *really* get knocked down? I am talking about those few devastating moments all of us have in our careers. A simple "it is what it is" is not enough to motivate me to get back up and jump back into the fight. I have found I need something more powerful during those times when it feels like the world is coming to an end. Fortunately, I found the perfect maxim a long time ago.

In eighth grade we were required to read *The Old Man and the Sea* by Ernest Hemingway. I liked it mostly because it was short and it was about fishing. At that age, you are not exactly seeking deep insight in the literature you are assigned to read. I remember reading along quickly when I came to the part where the old man was battling the fish and he was near complete exhaustion. At that point I read two sentences that have since changed my life on multiple occasions. Hemingway wrote,

> But man is not made for defeat. A man can be
> destroyed but not defeated.

I recall pausing and reading those lines over and over. They spoke to me.

Hemingway's words were my first personal maxim. I relied on those words to keep me going during the many times I considered dropping out of West Point because the experience there was difficult.

His words remind me that I can never give up, and the only way to prevent me from reaching my goal is to break me into a million little pieces. Those words consistently help me get back up and get back in the fight no matter how badly broken I may feel at that moment.

The Hemingway maxim saved my job at one point. I was assigned to a project that at first, was exciting and important. I was given the lead role on the project, and my work was highly visible to the most senior levels of the organization. As the project progressed, things got increasingly political. Turf wars erupted, and much of my day-to-day work became mindless recasting of spreadsheets. I began dreading going to the office every day because I knew I either was going to be a spreadsheet monkey or would be negotiating political treaties between warring factions within the company. It was not the most productive environment, to say the least.

I let my frustration get the best of me. I increasingly "checked out" mentally and disengaged from the content of the work. I began voicing my displeasure and frustrations, first with other members of the team and then more broadly with people in the organization. My attitude sucked, and my performance followed. I am not proud of my behavior on that project. I am embarrassed by it. My attitude got so bad I began making mistakes and making enemies. One day I voiced my frustrations in an unprofessional manner through a channel I believed was private. It wasn't. The next day there was a big meeting that included members of the project team and several senior executives. During the meeting one of the senior executives said they were going to take the project in a new direction, and they named one of my colleagues as the project lead. It took me a few moments to realize what had happened. I had essentially been fired as the project leader in a public forum. Granted, there was no mention of my responsibilities changing, but it was readily apparent to everyone in the room what had happened.

I was fit to be tied. My thoughts raced. *How dare they do this to me? After all I have done for the organization, they have no right to treat me this way.* The downward spiral of negativity began consuming me. At the bottom of that black vortex was the stark realization that my career trajectory in the organization had been fundamentally altered in a less-than-positive way. Heck, for all I knew that career path had come to an end, and I was essentially finished.

I gave myself the rest of the day off to regroup and think about things. As I contemplated the shattered pieces of my role, I remembered Hemingway's words. Defeat would mean acknowledging I had lost and given up the fight. Knowing that the loss of my responsibilities was self-inflicted made accepting defeat a reasonable decision. It would have been easy to do. I could have dusted off my resume and sought new employment elsewhere, but that would have meant I was accepting defeat. Hemingway reminded me that this was not a viable option for me.

By relying on my maxim to guide my behavior, I made the decision to get back to work the next day and begin producing the great work I knew I was capable of. It was not an easy task. It took me several months to get past the negative perception of me that I had created. There were many painful conversations about my past performance, and the quality of my work was continuously scrutinized. Frankly, I deserved all of it. Any time I faced those difficult moments, I remembered Hemingway's words and spurred myself onward. That is not to say I did not consider quitting multiple times. Every time I considered that option, however, Hemingway reminded me I could not make that choice.

Over time I once again proved I was a valuable contributor to the organization. I would always carry the scars from that project, but the wounds eventually healed, and people rarely remembered those times. Without this maxim I likely would have left the organization and accepted defeat. With it, I decided that in order for me to leave they would have to fire me, and I would perform in a manner such that they could never make that decision. This personal maxim got my career back on track.

Here is another example of a maxim's power. Maria, a senior manager who ran an accounting group, had a high-pressure role. Whenever budgets, earnings releases, tax filings, or any other event requiring financial reporting came up, she and her team would get slammed with work. There were many long hours and hectic days, but no matter how difficult things got, Maria was able to quickly recover from setbacks and crunches. She told me her maxim for picking herself up was "Two hundred hours in two weeks." She explained how, prior to her current job, she worked for an accounting firm that served major corporations and did a lot of work in support of mergers and acquisitions. During one particular crisis, Maria logged two hundred hours of work in a two-week period. It was exhausting, challenging, and frustrating work. She recalled, "I've never worked that hard in my life. I remember looking at my time sheet for that two-week period and I could not believe the number of hours I had spent at work. Now, whenever things get tough and it becomes crunch time, I just remember *two hundred hours in two weeks* and the work doesn't seem that hard. Thinking about that draining period in my career helps pick me up and remind me that I have been through worse times."

WRITING YOUR MAXIMS

Remember, maxims can come from anywhere. Mine came from a book I read in eighth grade and from a hallway conversation in which my boss reoriented my thinking. As you think about writing yours, be open to a variety of sources for the raw material. When you choose a phrase or image as your maxim, it should remind you of an emotionally powerful story in an instant. When you write the maxim, you need to make it as short as possible. Do not try to explain the entire story in the maxim itself; just provide the phrase or image that *reminds* you of the story. That phrase or image is the key that should unlock the memories and emotions tied to the story behind it.

Now it is your turn to create your maxim. Spend a few moments thinking about a challenge you faced and overcame. Review that difficult situation and try to recall the moment when you decided you were going to fight and win rather than simply give up. Once you've decided on a situation that has strong emotional resonance for you, answer the following questions about it:

- Is there anything like a quote, image, or song you associate with that moment?
- Where were you and who were you talking to when the incident happened? Did the other person say or do something that led you to overcome the challenge?
- If you were alone, do you remember what changed your mindset and got you to stand up and get over the obstacle?
- How do you pick yourself up during difficult times?
- Are there things you tell yourself or role models you think of when you have to climb out of whatever hole life throws you into?
- Is there a song, a story, or a poem that motivates you to overcome obstacles?

The trigger that reminds you of this incident and inspires you to overcome future challenges is your maxim. If you ever failed to make a sports team growing up, then practiced the entire year that followed and made the team the next season, your maxim might be something like "Making the baseball team—the second time around." Your maxim needs to remind you of how to face adversity and overcome it.

You may find that you want to create a couple of maxims, and they may apply to different situations. One may be focused on overcoming simple everyday obstacles, the other designed to help you during the most difficult life events that come your way. It is obviously up to you whether you choose to have one or two maxims. Either way, I highly encourage you to at least write the maxim designed to help you during those huge challenges that come your way. I hope you won't need to use it often, but when you do it will be there for you. Once you have a draft of these one or two maxims, step away from your work and come back to it in a day. If this maxim is designed to inspire you in the darkest of times, you had better be sure it is a compelling one. Ask yourself the following questions about the maxim to see how strong it is:

- Does this maxim inspire me?
- Is this a memory I can rely on to pick myself up when all seems lost?
- If I explained the story behind the maxim to members of my team, would they understand how I motivate myself in difficult times?

- Would thinking about this maxim have helped me through the most difficult times I've faced in the past?

Make sure you are satisfied that your maxims pass this test. If they do, write them down in Appendix B. The maxim or two you've created in this chapter will help you deal with difficult situations in a positive way. When you are faced with a crisis and your motivation is lacking, these maxims will give you the lift you need. The way you handle problems and crises will always be scrutinized by your team members— and if they see that your approach to handling it is effective, they will usually emulate it. They take their behavioral cues from you. If your maxims help put you in a positive frame of mind during those moments, they can have a strong positive impact on your performance and the performance of your team as well.

CHAPTER 8

[HOW DO YOU HOLD YOURSELF ACCOUNTABLE?]

Nothing gets done if no one is accountable for delivering the goods. One job you have as a leader is to ensure that tasks assigned to your team get carried out to the highest standards possible. You are also accountable for setting the tone of your organization and defining its culture. The way you personally approach accountability sets the standard for how you expect members of your team to behave. If you consistently sidestep being accountable for results, do not be surprised when your team does the same. If instead you hold yourself accountable, you have a performance standard you can hold up in front of your team. When you achieve that standard it gives you the moral high ground to demand similar performance from members of your organization. All accountability starts with you—the leader.

SETTING THE STANDARD FOR ACCOUNTABILITY

You may have a boss who helps define your assignments. You may be an entrepreneur who must identify and execute the assignments on your own. Either way, accountability is at the heart of execution. Failure to define accountability leads to missed assignments, sloppy work, and lost opportunities. Its absence creates unhealthy finger-pointing dynamics whereby everyone else is to blame except the person pointing the fingers. If you as a leader are pointing fingers at others for their failures, you are likely just as responsible for the failure as they are. Moving yourself to this way of thinking will help shift you toward being a more responsible leader.

Being a leader requires a shift from a mindset of someone else holding us accountable to a position of holding ourselves accountable. By making this shift we move to the powerful place known as *being responsible*. The great thing about leading yourself and being responsible is that when something goes wrong you do not have to look far to find the problem—you have only yourself to blame.

Now, none of us likes to fail. Most of the time we will avoid failure at all costs. One way to avoid failure is to blame others for something not working. "We didn't get the project done because IT did not give us enough resources to do it on time." Does that sound painfully familiar? It is easy to blame someone else, thereby absolving ourselves of blame for the failure. This is known as taking the low road. What if, in this situation, our boss was still going to hold us accountable for the project's failure regardless of whose fault it was? We might act differently and figure out a way to get the resources we need or change the scope of the project so we can succeed. Our own fear of failure becomes a great motivator for us to do what we know needs to get done. My question is, why are we, as leaders, waiting for someone else to hold us accountable for the result? Why don't we save a step and hold ourselves accountable? We must overcome the fear of failure and avoid the blame game.

Many managers (which I differentiate from leaders) understand they are accountable, but few make the leap to being responsible. Accountability is simply being the first person called when things get screwed up. Responsibility is about ownership and fixing things before that phone call comes in. There is a big difference between the two.

Responsible leaders assign themselves tasks and hold themselves accountable for delivering the results. They do not wait for their boss or their customer to ask for results—they deliver the results proactively and resolve issues without being told what to do. Responsible leaders make things happen. This difference between accountability and responsibility is one of the differentiators between managers and leaders. I will discuss more of these differences in greater depth in later chapters.

Many of us are responsible leaders but occasionally revert to the blame game or abdicate responsibility entirely. Responsibility brings pressure. Pressure is uncomfortable. The easiest way to remove that source of discomfort is to let ourselves off the hook for being accountable for an outcome. It is during those difficult times that a leadership maxim focused on accountability and responsibility can keep you on track. When you step up to the pressure and face it head-on, you make the giant leap from being accountable to being responsible. You cross over the line separating managers from leaders.

A maxim that consistently reminds you to hold yourself accountable for results will help you make the shift to being a responsible leader. My maxim for doing this consists of six words:

I see it, I own it.

This maxim forces me to find a resolution for problems I come across (or problems I cause, for that matter). Whether I am accountable for the result or not, if I see a problem or opportunity, I need to take responsibility for driving the outcome. Let me be clear: I am not advocating taking on responsibility for delivering every result in the organization. I am simply holding myself accountable for ensuring that *someone* delivers that result. If I see a problem in another department, this maxim leads me to take action. That does not necessarily mean I personally fix that problem. My ownership of it could be as simple as letting a peer know he has a problem he needs to resolve in his department. Contrast this approach with seeing a problem and ignoring it, with the justification of "Well, that's not *my* department, so I don't have to fix it."

This maxim drives my behavior from issues as simple as picking up trash on my corporate campus to those as important as seeing bad behavior in someone else's group and taking it upon myself to correct it. This maxim is my nagging conscience that gnaws at me if I walk past a problem I know I should fix.

I have used this maxim for many years, and now it is ingrained in my thinking. When I was on a business trip in Dublin, Ireland, I had some rare free time and took a stroll through a city park. I walked by some fast-food trash someone had thrown on the grass. I did not pick it up. Almost six months later it still bothers me that I was too lazy to take three steps out of my way and dispose of that trash properly. Was I accountable for keeping the park clean? No. But as a leader, having a mindset that I see myself as responsible for solving problems, picking it up would have been consistent with my internal beliefs.

I am not trying to turn you into a trash collector. I am trying to get you to proactively take responsibility for the organization around you. Small tasks like trash pickup are indicators of how responsible you are as an owner of the organization you lead.

My "I see it, I own it" maxim has led me to take some drastic actions on occasion. When I was responsible for all the technology infrastructure for my business unit, my team was charged with implementing a new technology platform across all our locations. The first system "go live" implementation was to occur at our biggest location during the site's busiest month. As the cutover to the new system approached, I began receiving conflicting status reports from IT, our vendors, and my team. Two days before the "go live," it was obvious we were far behind schedule, and it was becoming clear that we would not get the system installed on time. I told IT they had until the close of business to get me a satisfactory status report and contingency plan, or I was going to have to do it myself. Doing it myself would include making a site visit, which would require flying to that location.

Close of business came and went without a status report.

The next morning, IT began getting frantic calls from our technology vendor that some company executive was at the site asking the installation team all sorts of questions. IT said they did not know who it was and told the vendor they would figure out what was going on. The vendor was getting upset that someone from our company was directing their personnel without their knowledge or approval. When IT called my desk, they got my voicemail. They tried my cell phone, and I immediately picked up.

"Hey, our vendor is saying some exec from our side is at the location telling their people what to do. They're pretty upset. Is one of your team members at the location or something?"

My response: "No. *I'm* here."

There was dead silence on the other end of the line. A few moments later came a hesitant "Oh. Um. Why are you there?"

I responded that things were not getting done. I had given both IT and the vendor plenty of opportunities to get things moving and give me accurate reports. Because I was accountable for delivery of results, and I was not planning on playing a blame game when we did not cut over on time, I had taken it upon myself to go to the site and make things happen.

Despite my best efforts, we cut over one day late. However, had I not gotten on a 6:00 A.M. flight to our location, we would have been a *week* late.

I did not ask my boss whether I should or could go. I saw the problem, and I owned fixing it. Sure, I ruffled a few feathers in the process, but in the end the most important thing was getting our site cut over so they could go about their business. The site was my customer. They did not want to hear excuses from me about IT, vendors, or any other reason their system was not installed on time. They wanted results, and I took personal responsibility for delivering exactly that. It would have been easy for me to stay home and do the best I could to resolve the problem from my desk, but my maxim pushed me to be more accountable for the result. When I looked at this problem in the context of my maxim, there was really only one choice

I could make that would enable me to live up to the standard I set for myself. My maxim changed my behavior and led me to take a more active role in solving the problem I saw.

A client of mine had an interesting maxim for holding herself accountable. Jillian recalled a story about a time she stepped up to a very difficult situation and did what she knew was the right thing. "I had a woman on my team who was a fantastic performer. Her work was always stellar, but over a six-month period, her work deteriorated. She was late. Her quality was poor. Her attitude was less than enthusiastic. It was difficult for me to see this happen because she was also a good friend of mine."

Jillian gave the woman a few months to turn her work around. She gave her candid and direct feedback, which was painful for Jillian to do due to their friendship. Unfortunately, the woman's performance did not improve.

"The day came when it became clear she simply wasn't going to return to her previous levels of high performance and I had to let her go. Ugh. The notion of firing someone I was also friends with was unbearable, but it was even more painful to think about prolonging a terrible situation. I let her go. There were tears, but she said she understood, and she apologized for putting me in a position where I had to make such a decision."

As Jillian related this story, it was clear how emotionally charged those events were for her.

She continued, "Several years after laying her off, I ran into her at a store. She told me how getting fired was one of the best things that ever happened to her. She thanked me profusely for making the decision, because she said it forced her to get her life in order. At the time I fired her she was having all sorts of personal problems, and losing her job gave her time to work them out. She eventually found another job that she loved. It was hard for me to understand how so much good came out of such a painful situation. This story reminds me how being responsible as a leader sometimes means making painfully difficult decisions, but those decisions can have positive effects down the road. My maxim for being responsible is 'Sometimes you have to fire your friends.' It reminds me that my role requires me to make tough choices."

WRITING YOUR MAXIMS

Now that you understand how *I* hold myself responsible, how will you define a maxim that will help *you* move from being accountable to being responsible? It needs to be something that drives you to action and keeps you from laying blame at the feet of others. You are trying to write a maxim that pushes you to always be a take-charge type of leader. It is designed to prevent you from ever saying the words *That's not my job*. This maxim needs to shift your bias from observing to acting, regardless of the situation in which you find yourself. Here are a few questions to get you started:

- Have you ever taken charge of something not directly assigned to you, after which your involvement helped drive a successful outcome?
- Have you ever seen a problem before anyone else noticed it and then fixed it without anyone telling you to?
- Have you ever seen a problem, not taken responsibility for it, and regretted it later?
- How do you keep yourself from playing the blame game?
- How do you convince yourself to do what you know is right rather than doing what is easy?
- How do you maintain a sense of ownership and a bias toward taking action?

Again, do not feel limited to only answering these questions. Write down all the thoughts, images, phrases, and sayings that come to you as you consider the answers. Think about the stories behind those phrases. For example, if you recall your father saying something like "When you point a finger, three fingers point back at you," that might be your maxim. A lesson passed on by a parent is likely to carry strong emotions with it. Write down your reminders of how you will hold yourself accountable. Step away from your work for a meaningful amount of time, then review it. Which stories and phrases resonate with you? Which ones do you get excited about? Simplify the phrase that embodies the story, and you'll have a draft maxim.

To determine whether the maxim you wrote will effectively hold you accountable and drive you to take ownership for things around you, see how it stacks up against the following questions:

- Will this maxim encourage me to improve the world around me even if those improvements are outside of my defined responsibilities?
- If I find myself playing the blame game, will this maxim refocus me on becoming part of the solution rather than wasting time and energy trying to determine who is at fault?
- Will this maxim direct me toward choosing the harder right over the easier wrong?

When you are comfortable that your maxim holds up to these questions, document it in Appendix B. If your maxim can get you to make hard choices and take ownership for the state of the world around you, it will help you be the accountable leader you aspire to be. Eventually that ownership will enable you to make the shift from accountability to responsibility. If, however, the maxim cannot withstand these questions, take some time to figure out how you can make it stronger. Do not stop refining it until you are convinced that it can change your behavior during moments when you are faced with difficult choices.

The shift from accountability to responsibility is a big one. It requires an entirely new mindset, and your behaviors need to demonstrate that new way of thinking on a regular basis. Writing a maxim designed to consistently keep you thinking about how to act responsibly will help you remember to proactively seek to improve the world around you. That bias will shine through in your actions, and it will set a powerful example for the members of your team to emulate. If you follow the guidance of the maxim frequently enough, you will find you've left the blame game far behind you.

Congratulations! You now have a preliminary set of leadership maxims for how you are going to lead yourself. If you have written them well, they will guide your behavior in difficult situations and keep you focused on doing the kind of work you enjoy doing. These maxims will remind you where you are headed in life and will help you get there with your integrity intact.

PART 3

[LEADING THE THINKING]

CHAPTER 9

[BECOMING A THOUGHT LEADER]

Once you have defined how you will lead yourself, you need to create some maxims to get you looking forward and to set new directions for your organization. The status quo is never good enough. I cannot think of a single successful leader I have ever met whose strategy was *Don't change a thing! Everything is perfect!* In fact, the best leaders I have worked with continuously challenge the thinking, blow up business models, and question how they can get their organization to a better place. This is what leading the thinking is all about.

THE IMPORTANCE OF LEADING THE THINKING

When you focus on leading the thinking you will see new trends, opportunities, and risks before your competitors see them. You can shape the market rather than having the market shape you. You might uncover huge new breakthrough opportunities that get your team excited and energized about their work. But the only way you can see these things is to dedicate time and energy to thinking about them.

The importance of leading the thinking was driven home for me on a consulting project. I was responsible for leading the team and coming up with new growth ideas for the client. I focused most of my energy on the hard-core analytics and the creation of the presentations that the team and I were delivering to the client. The models we built and the presentations we wrote were powerful and beautiful. When the team had a momentary break of a few days with some relative down time, the senior consulting partner on the team requested we all get together for some group problem solving. She asked me to bring our top new growth ideas to the meeting for discussion.

While presenting to the senior consulting partner during that meeting I mindlessly regurgitated some ideas an industry expert had provided us with. The ideas sounded really cool. They were about building new technology-driven marketplaces, connecting remote sources of data and aggregating them, selling new analytical insights to different industry sectors, and all sorts of other sexy ideas. In my mind I had led the team to come up with some great new businesses.

That is when the pain started. The senior partner started asking me questions about the ideas. She was genuinely excited and wanted to learn more about them. As she asked more questions, I found myself frequently saying, "Well, the industry expert said . . ." It became abundantly clear that none of these ideas involved any original thinking on my part. That part was OK, because we had been taught to find the best ideas in our firm and see how we could apply them to our client's situation. It was the latter part, about "applying them," that got me in trouble. As the partner asked questions, I began to see all the gaps in my thinking. I had not considered many of the logical implications of the ideas we were recommending. Unfortunately, I had not done my job, and none of my unoriginal ideas were even remotely executable.

Had I done my job better, I would have led the team to consider all the questions the partner was asking. Her questions were well-intentioned and, upon reflection, pretty obvious. I was extremely frustrated that I had missed thinking about them. I had been so absorbed in the day-to-day activities of the team that I had not carved out the required "think time" to identify the questions I should have been asking. Needless to say, I was sent away from that meeting with pointed guidance to "go think about the problem a little harder and come back when you have put some deeper thought into these ideas." That was the day I learned what it means to lead the thinking.

HOW TO BECOME A THOUGHT LEADER

The higher you rise in your organization, the less doing and the more thinking you are expected to do. You do not get paid the big bucks to make the widgets. You get paid to think about whether you should be making widgets at all and, if so, where the most attractive markets are for your particular kind of widget.

Going from being a doer to being a thinker is a big leap. It requires you to let go of always being the person with the answers and to instead become the person asking the questions. This transition can be extremely uncomfortable. Fortunately, it is not an impossible shift as long as you focus your thoughts beyond the day-to-day tasks at hand.

As we enter organizations and rise through the ranks, we are trained and expected to have the answers. We, after all, are the front line. We do the work. When someone more senior asks us for information, our job description is to provide it. And provide it we do. We become experts in our field. We know all the answers. This is how we earn the reputation of being the go-to person on the team. Unfortunately, the answers are usually all about what has already happened.

To gain new knowledge, we need to ask questions, not just provide answers. It is questions that lead us to insights. Sure, sometimes simple questions can lead to interesting answers, but more often than not it is the questions that arise when someone takes a step back from the day-to-day minutiae that generate new insights. You gain the most knowledge by making connections, seeing trends, predicting the future, or looking at things others have ignored. Think about the smartest senior executives you work with. Do they ask more questions or provide more answers? I will bet you find the smarter ones ask a lot of great questions and the weaker executives lean toward providing all the answers.

Think about all the wonderful new insights you can lead your team to by simply asking the right questions. Consider the positive impact you can have on your bottom line if you can convince people to look at the world differently and pursue creative new opportunities. How great would it be if you could paint a future vision of the business and set performance expectations for your team such that your biggest challenge becomes getting out of their way so they can execute the brilliant new plan?

WHERE TO START

To do all these great things, you need to establish some maxims that will force you to think about new opportunities and set a vision for where you are headed. Your maxims will be designed to help you look at the world from new and different perspectives. They will help you break out of the stagnant thinking pervasive in many organizations; they will set expectations for your team about where you want them to go and how you expect them to behave along the way. If you write these maxims well, they will routinely take you to a place where you are asking the right questions, articulating a compelling vision, and taking action to achieve that vision.

Beyond simply articulating your maxims, you need to change your behaviors and how you allocate your time. To successfully lead the thinking, you must set aside some "think time" every month (half a day at the very least) to take a step back and evaluate how you are thinking about the business. By creating these maxims and dedicating some thinking time, you can take the organization well beyond where you once thought it could go.

I have asked many leaders I have worked with to define thought leadership. More often than not, they spout empty clichés—phrases like "think outside the box," "push the envelope," "break the paradigm," and "step-change improvement." What *exactly* do these tired phrases mean? More important, how do you actually do these things?

Let's talk about thought leadership in real terms. The term *thought leader*, as we define it in our firm, is as follows:

A thought leader is someone who delivers business results by agitating for and leading change.

Thomas Edison succinctly stated, "Vision without execution is a hallucination." Thought leadership and leading the thinking is not only about having brilliant ideas. It is also about driving them to action. Great leaders make their ideas tangible and executable. As you begin articulating your leading-the-thinking maxims, you need to explore both of these concepts: ideas and execution.

The following questions can help you explore how you will lead the thinking. Through this part of the process, you will define your own leadership maxims that serve as daily reminders to push the thinking beyond "that's how we've always done it." You need to lead your team to a better tomorrow you have helped define. To that end:

- What standards do you hold your team to?
- Where are you taking your people?
- How will you foresee the future?
- After all that thinking, how will you drive action?

The leading-the-thinking maxims you define will get you to look at problems differently. They should shake you from your usual daily routine and help you lead your organization beyond business as usual.

Leading the thinking is difficult to do. First, it requires that we break away from daily execution and operations. That is hard because the results of operations are immediate, tangible, and important. Second, when leading the thinking, we have to ask challenging questions and deal with ambiguous problems. Those are not easy skills to master. Writing maxims focused on leading the thinking will help you step outside your organization's present challenges and enable you to look longer term at where you are trying to go and what you are trying to become as a company. You will be building the foundation for all the actions your team will take, because that foundation is the desired future state of your organization. Your leading-the-thinking maxims will spur you to define a compelling future vision and encourage you to continuously be on the lookout for new threats and opportunities. By leading the thinking, you can avoid the disaster of one day waking up to find that your business has become irrelevant as the world changed around it and evolved beyond it.

CHAPTER 10

[WHAT STANDARDS DO YOU HOLD YOUR TEAM TO?]

As you created maxims to guide your own behavior when you defined how you will lead yourself, you also need to provide maxims concerning performance standards for your team. These standards can be focused on anything from how you treat customers to how you uphold team values; ideally, they will point your team clearly in the direction in which you want them to go. They keep you and your team on track and ensure that quality remains high as all of you head toward your goals. By creating standards you eliminate confusion as to how you want your team members to behave. Those standards help ensure that the actions your team takes are consistent with the vision of what you want your organization to become. This clarity also reduces confusion and inefficiency caused by members of your team trying to figure out your expectations of them. If you can clarify your expectations quickly and simply, they can spend their energy on executing the plan rather than on figuring out what your standards are.

DEFINING THE STANDARDS

As you create your maxims that define your standards, you will likely find them to be both internally and externally focused. The internally focused maxims will be more a reflection of your beliefs as a leader in general. They will translate to almost any team you lead over the course of your career, irrespective of your role, function, or industry. They are typically focused on the internal workings of your team and how you expect your people to interact with you. The externally focused maxims will be more a function of your team's environment and responsibilities. These might center on customer service, safety, quality, or any other critical aspect of your team's being distinctive at what they do on a day-to-day basis. Your environmentally driven external maxims should home in on the one thing you want your team to focus on more than anything else.

I have used many internally and externally focused maxims over the years. They have changed over time, because either my team was different and I had different expectations of them based on their capabilities or the environment in which we were working was different. Here are some maxims that I and other leaders I know have used:

In God we trust. All others bring data.

A cadet will not lie, cheat, or steal nor tolerate those who do.

Is this right for the customer?

The first maxim—"In God we trust. All others bring data"—is an internally focused maxim a client used to effectively direct the behaviors of his team. It defines the standard Shirish used for making decisions. He was an executive at a small technology company, and his team regularly launched new consumer-focused initiatives. There were many times his team members would go to Shirish with recommendations for new products or features. At first blush the ideas all sounded great, but he was managing a complex business. Over the years he had seen multiple occasions when an obvious and logical answer was absolutely wrong because his customers behaved in unexpected ways. There were several instances when he had approved a recommendation from the team because it was logical, only to later learn that they had wasted a substantial amount of time and money, because the outcomes were exactly the opposite of what everyone had predicted would happen.

Eventually Shirish adopted the maxim "In God we trust. All others bring data." Any time a team member came to him with a new idea, he would point to his whiteboard where this maxim was written. "It sounds like a good idea," he would say, "but do you have any data to support going in that direction?"

This mantra became a performance standard for his people. They knew that every time they went to him with a recommendation that would affect customers, they needed to bring him some form of data validating why it was a good idea. He was always supportive of acting on the idea if they brought data and made their case. This maxim became the performance standard to which Shirish held his team. He had to point to the whiteboard less and less frequently because over time they learned that this was his expectation. Eventually the maxim changed the behavior of the team.

There was, however, a downside he had to manage. After pointing to the "bring data" part of the maxim for many months, Shirish began finding his team coming to him with extensive amounts of data and analysis. More often than not it was overkill. He had emphasized the maxim so much that he began getting too much of a good thing. Now that he had his team bringing data, he had to moderate their behavior and let them know when to back off the data as well. He regularly found himself balancing how much information he asked for, in order to achieve the right mix of rigor and efficiency. Sometimes a maxim can encourage too much of the behavior you desire. He understood that dynamic and managed it by explaining why it was the standard—and also pointing out when he thought the team was exceeding the standard. The maxim served him well because it clearly told his team what he expected of them whenever they made a decision: *be sure to have some data to back up your idea before you act.* After hearing Shirish tell the story behind his maxim, I immediately adopted it as one of my own, because I too faced challenges similar to the ones he did, and the concept resonated for me.

The second maxim is also internally focused: "A cadet will not lie, cheat, or steal nor tolerate those who do." It is the West Point cadet honor code. I learned it on my first day at the academy.

The first part of it is straightforward. It directs an individual's behavior. The last clause about toleration is where the power of the code resides. A cadet could be kicked out of the academy for violating any part of the code. If you lied? Gone. If you cheated? Gone. Stole? Gone. Saw someone who did any of those three things and did not either ask them to turn themselves in or turn them in yourself? Gone. The toleration clause created a strong code-reinforcing mechanism that taught us it was unacceptable to turn a blind eye to someone else's breaking of the code. It stated that we were as dishonorable as the person telling the lie if we simply ignored the transgression. The code focused internally on our organization as a corps of cadets and set a clear standard for our behavior.

After four years of living under that code, it took on strong personal meaning for me. At first I lived in fear of it. As I grew as a leader, I learned to respect the code and took a great deal of pride in my ability to live up to that lofty standard. It has been a leadership maxim of mine since the day I graduated. I ask members of my team to aspire to that standard. Since graduating, I have on occasion failed to live up to that standard myself. No, I have never stolen anything or cheated customers or business partners, but I have lied. In the moment the lie seemed small. On other occasions I rationalized the lie away and made excuses for why it was okay to lie in that particular situation. After those events, and upon reflection on this maxim, I felt a profound sense of disappointment in myself for having violated it. It is excruciating to sit here and write these words, disclosing to thousands of strangers how I have deceived others and failed to live up to what is now a self-imposed standard. Yes, I have fessed up to the times I have lied, and I have taken my well-deserved lumps. The worst lumps, though, are the ones I give myself as I reflect on my behavior and accept my failures.

Given the depth of this particular maxim, let's take a moment to step back and see how powerful the leadership maxims approach can be. Imagine you are a member of my team. I tell you that a personal maxim of mine is to "not lie, cheat, or steal nor tolerate those who do." When you hear that, you nod and say "That makes sense." Then I tell you the story behind the code. I tell you what it means to me personally. I share how I have violated the code in the past (after graduating from West Point) and how terrible it has made me feel when I have done that. That conversation gets very deep very fast. You know a heck of a lot more about me and what I am made of after you hear my story. I hope you have gained a degree of respect for my candor and authenticity in admitting I have failed to live up to my self-imposed standard. Ideally you feel an increased sense of trust between us because I was willing to expose something unattractive about myself, trusting that you would not judge me or think poorly of me for my failures. A good maxim does all of these things. It exposes who you are as a person. It helps you share your beliefs. It is a vehicle to tell your story. It builds understanding, trust, and respect between the leader and those he or she seeks to influence. Would you rather follow a leader who admits to fallibility but seeks to achieve the highest standards, or the leader who speaks in broad platitudes and proclaims to have never made a mistake? The answer is pretty easy. Maxims are a tool for demonstrating you are that former leader. They are not easy to write but the investment of time and energy is worth it.

The third of these maxims is externally focused. It is an example of how a leader expected her team to interact with individuals outside of that team. It is how I saw a call center manager direct her associates to treat her customers. Vikki regularly told her team that when faced with a choice of what to do in any situation, they should simply ask "Is this right for the customer?" After asking that, the right action would become abundantly clear. Every week in team meetings she would reinforce this phrase. She explained the maxim to all new hires on their first day of work and told them how she wanted that question to govern their behavior. Any time someone from her team came to ask Vikki what to do in a particular customer situation, she would ask "Is that right for the customer?" If the answer was yes, she told the team member to go make it happen. If the answer was no, she asked that team member what would be right for the customer in that situation, then she directed them to do that instead. Her maxim became an ingrained part of the organization's culture.

Vikki gave her people a standard of behavior. She avoided doing what I have seen many call center leaders do. All too often I have encountered call centers where the managers give their people laundry lists of proscriptive rules to cover every situation in which they might find themselves. Not only is that an inefficient approach, but it does not create a positive work culture. In contrast, Vikki empowered her associates to make decisions. As long as they were trying to adhere to the maxim, they were doing what she wanted them to do.

Sometimes Vikki's associates went too far with the maxim and did *really* right for the customer. There were some occasions where doing right for the customer would have entailed waiving a late fee on the customer's account. Some associates did *really* right for the customer by waiving multiple fees when waiving one fee would have been sufficient. Yes, the associates were doing right by the customer and following Vikki's guidance, but they were not making the best decisions possible. Those became coaching moments for Vikki. She never discouraged the behavior of trying to do right by the customer. Instead, she focused her coaching on helping the associate understand how to balance the objectives of doing right by the customer while keeping the objectives of the business in mind. Her use of this maxim created a clear expectation for her team and built a customer-focused culture like no other I have ever seen. The surprising part was that Vikki was responsible for a credit card collections call center! Her team's morale was always high, she always hit her numbers, and, oddly enough, customers liked dealing with members of her team even though they were in collections. The real value of this maxim became clear when customers said they wanted to pay off their balance with her company before they paid off balances with other creditors because her team understood the customers' problems and did what they could to help their situations. After seeing the impact of this simple maxim, I stole it—and I have used it on multiple occasions in jobs I held after working at that credit card company. The maxim had the same impact for me in those roles as it did for Vikki in her collections group. (Yes, it's OK to steal maxims; in fact, it's highly recommended as long as that maxim resonates for you!)

WRITING YOUR MAXIMS

Now it is your turn. You need to articulate your standards of performance and put guidelines in place for your team members. To generate a leadership maxim to explain your standards, ask yourself, "How do I want my team behaving when I am not there to give guidance? What are my expectations for how they perform?" You also need to set expectations for how you want them to deal with you, as well as what you want them to focus on as they deal with others. Remember, you need to create maxims with deep personal meaning for you, in the same way that the cadet honor code has meaning for me.

Here are some questions to get you started on writing your maxim:

- What are your expectations regarding your team's standards of behavior?
- What do you expect of your team every day?
- How do you want them to interact with you?
- How do you want your team behaving when you are not around?
- Has someone important in your life ever set a high standard for you that you either met or failed to meet? How did they articulate that standard?
- How can you articulate your high standards of performance in a simple phrase or with an image that conveys your personal beliefs around those standards?
- What is the most critical objective you want your team to achieve (customer service, quality, safety, efficiency)? Is there a simple and personally meaningful way you can remind them of that objective?

Write down the first thoughts and images that come to mind. Try to capture phrases, sayings, stories, and ideas that evoke strong emotions for you. Then set your work down for a while. When you come back to it, which of those stories or sayings leap off the page at you? Try to distill those ideas to their bare essentials. For example, if you always ask your team to inform you of problems as soon as they arise, your maxim might be "Bad news ages poorly"—especially if you can clearly remember a situation in which you were not informed of a problem early and the outcome was painful.

In this maxim you are articulating the most important standards you want your team members to meet. Try to pick at least one internally focused maxim and one externally focused maxim. Once you have some maxims you think work for you, you need to test how strong they are. Ask yourself:

- Does the story behind this maxim have deep personal meaning to me? Is it free and clear of all buzzwords and B.S.?
- If I told someone on my team this maxim and they were in a difficult situation, would they clearly know what I would want them to do?
- If my team continuously adheres to this maxim, will it create the organizational culture I desire?
- Will consistent adherence to this maxim help my team achieve our goals without compromising our standards?

If the answers to all of those questions are "yes," you have a great start on some maxims that will establish the standards your team needs to meet. Write them down in Appendix B. As you use each maxim regularly, you will find better ways to articulate it, and you will build up a library of example situations in which it did or did not work. You can share those stories with your team to help them better understand what your standards and expectations are.

The maxims that define your standards are critical for driving alignment and managing expectations for your team. You are letting them know how you want them to behave, which in turn empowers them and gives them the ability to operate freely while acting in a way that is consistent with your goals. As you move from one role to the next, you may need to change your maxims, but regardless of where you work, your team will always require guidance on what your standards are. When you articulate those standards clearly and concisely, you reduce confusion and help people focus on what you consider to be important. Once you have articulated those standards, you next need to let your team know where you are going.

CHAPTER 11

[
WHERE ARE YOU TAKING YOUR PEOPLE?
]

The only things more painful to read than most corporate mission statements are corporate vision statements. Many vision statements are written by committee. They start out direct, clear, and compelling, but as everyone involved has their turn at contributing their input, those visions lose their luster. The direct parts of the vision get watered down so as not to offend, exclude, or intimidate people. Also, items are added to the vision statement because people want to ensure that their pet function or goal is included, and this lengthens the document and makes it more confusing.

Eventually some vision statements come to look more like a bill that has moved through Congress, to which everyone involved has tacked on their personal amendment, than they do a compelling articulation of what the organization will be in the future. This occurs because too much gets included in the statement and too little is said. These vision statements fill complete pages with buzzwords but don't actually say anything worthwhile and therefore cannot clearly drive action. And if a vision statement cannot drive action, it is not worth the paper it is printed on. Pythagoras said, "Do not say a little in many words but a great deal in a few." Leaders who write vision statements would do well to heed his advice. How is anyone supposed to get excited about a page full of blathering buzzwords describing a future full of meaningless phrases? I am not saying *all* corporate, business unit, or team vision statements are bad. There are some fantastic ones out there. Unfortunately, there are more bad ones than good ones.

Before you go skipping this chapter with the excuse that you do not write vision statements at the corporate level, you must realize that you are responsible for setting the direction for your team. You as a leader must create a vision statement for your team when your team is large enough to warrant having one, so sit down and read. Any team that is responsible for a discrete organizational function should have a vision statement. It doesn't matter whether that team is as small as five people or as large as five thousand. You can write a powerful vision statement as long as all members of that team are focused on reaching the same goals in the same functional area. If your team is small or part of a larger discrete unit, it may not make sense to craft your own separate vision statement, but you still need to provide a vision statement for that team. This might mean adopting the vision statement of the next higher level organization.

SETTING A DIRECTION FOR YOUR TEAM

Whatever your situation or your title happens to be, the simple fact remains—you need to articulate a vision for the future state of your organization. We usually leave this up to the C-suite, but writing a vision statement at any level is a powerful exercise. Your people want to be excited to come to work. They want to be part of something bigger than they are. If you can paint a compelling future picture for them, they will be more excited to follow you to that destination. If you do not paint that picture, they are likely following you out of laziness or just morbid curiosity to see what is going to happen. The earlier in your career you learn how to create vision statements, the more successful you will be at writing them as your responsibilities expand. Think of this chapter as giving yourself a jump start toward being the architect of your company's future.

When written well, a vision statement can and should be one of your leadership maxims—that is, your vision maxim. But out of all your leadership maxims, this one will change the most frequently. It could change every time you take on a new role or move to a new organization. When you enter an organization that does not have a vision statement, you can set a clear direction for your team by creating one. If your organization does have a vision statement when you arrive, review it with a careful eye and ensure that the future it articulates is where you want to take your people. If it does, adopt it as your own maxim. If it does not, you are responsible for modifying it as you see fit or changing it entirely to suit your team. After all, you are the person navigating your team to your organization's destination. Your job is to define the destination, the path, and the guidelines. It is your team's job to get you there. When you articulate your vision maxim, you must be sure you are comfortable with the destination and the directions you are giving your people.

Writing a vision statement requires a great deal of thought and an ability to step outside of your daily grind and into a time beyond the foreseeable future. You need to make it concise, and it must clearly explain how your organization creates value. This value creation component is easier to articulate than you might think. Ask yourself *What will the business outcomes and results be if I achieve this component of my vision maxim?* Your vision maxim will comprise several key phrases, and you should be able to link each phrase to a desired business outcome. The following is my current vision maxim and the explanation behind it by way of example.

For my organization, the vision and corresponding maxim is

To become a global firm of uniquely skilled executives
who teach managers around the world how to be great leaders.

Is this aspirational? Absolutely. Is it possible? We are already making it happen—but not without a lot of hard work and focus. Let me break this vision maxim down into components and explain what each piece means to my organization. For each component phrase of the vision maxim, I will explain the desired business outcomes I expect to achieve if we attain these goals. Reading the real-world example of how we created our vision maxim should help you create a vision maxim of your own.

Let's look at the first part of my vision maxim: "To become a global firm of uniquely skilled executives." I lead a small leadership training firm that started out as a one-man shop. Over time I have added more highly talented people to the team. Having the phrase "unique executives" in our vision maxim keeps our focus on bringing in a specific type of leader to serve as one of our instructors. Our instructors are unique because each and every one has ten to twenty years of business experience as an executive at leading companies. While keeping their day jobs, they essentially serve as adjunct faculty members for our firm. The specific types of instructors we bring on must be credible leaders in industry and must also have deep expertise in the area of instruction in which they train our clients.

We conduct training sessions on topics like strategic planning, innovation, problem solving, decision making, executive communications, and, of course, leadership. We create all our own training content because we want to ensure that our offerings are available only from our firm. Were we to hire a large number of instructors who are "career trainers" rather than actual practitioners, we might compromise the real-world experience aspect of the value we deliver to clients. If we offer commodity training that can be purchased from hundreds, if not thousands, of other firms, then our offerings would be undifferentiated in the market. Our clients see our instructors' real-world experience as a key source of their credibility and benefit greatly from the fact that our courses are designed with the real world in mind.

As for achieving a vision of being global, we are. If the notion of a boutique training firm trying to go global seems audacious, it is. But again, a vision statement is supposed to drive action and get your team to reach for lofty goals. The vision statement helps you and your team keep your eyes open for opportunities you might otherwise miss. For example, when we first started writing the *thought*LEADERS blog (http://www.thoughtleadersllc.com/blog), we viewed it as a resource that we would refer clients to so they could read our thoughts on leadership topics, but we did not have a global component in our vision statement.

Since we added a global view, we have used the blog to find and take advantage of many opportunities to spread our perspectives around the world. As of this writing, we have had visitors from 168 countries read our work on our blog. We have had articles reprinted and translated in multiple countries, including France, Norway, Korea, and Bahrain. We have found opportunities to work with our clients at their international locations, including Hungary, Ireland, Vietnam, and Colombia. We have also taught leaders from many countries at training sessions here in the United States, effectively exporting our methods back to their home countries. Does this mean we are a global behemoth? Not by a long shot. But the maxim does lead us to evaluate and pursue a broader set of opportunities than we might have otherwise considered. The result of taking such a view is that our firm continues to grow in terms of both revenues and capabilities. We included this global component in the vision statement because we know leaders are facing increasingly high global pressures. Diversity of backgrounds, technology shifts, and economic interdependencies make it more critical than ever for leaders to understand and effectively operate in a global environment. By expanding our view to the global arena, we are better able to teach these leaders new skills in a classroom environment that incorporates a global perspective. The net result is that we provide a better and more valuable service to our clients than we would if we restricted ourselves to a domestic focus.

The second part of my vision maxim, "teaching managers around the world how to be great leaders," is at the core of what we do and what we aspire to be. I've touched on the difference between managers and leaders and will go into more detail in later chapters, but Admiral Grace Murray Hopper said it best when she stated "You manage things; you lead people." We aspire to always teach content and skills focused on leadership. Sure, some of the courses we teach center around management skills. When we teach those subjects, we always try to link the management aspect of the skill to how it can help people be better leaders too. The outcome of including this component in our vision maxim is that it keeps us true to the type of teaching we are good at and that our clients value quite highly. It reinforces our need to hire only instructors who are business executives and leaders themselves rather than hiring academicians or "career trainers." This approach also means that our pricing remains strong and we stay away from excessively competitive, crowded, and commoditized training service markets.

Now that you understand how we created our vision maxim, I would like you to evaluate how powerful it can be as a leadership tool. Imagine you were a potential instructor or possibly even a prospective client of our services. When you ask what we are about as a company, I could tell you "We aspire to become a global firm of uniquely skilled executives who teach managers around the world how to be great leaders." Would you understand who we are, what we do, and why we do it? Would you be excited about joining a team building toward that vision statement? Would you be interested in becoming a client who could benefit from our perspectives and unique capabilities? Our maxim was crafted to ensure that the answers to all of those questions will be "yes!"

What if you said you were interested but you wanted to learn more before you made a decision, and I told you the story and beliefs behind the maxim? Does that story give you a better understanding of me as a leader? Do you have a clear picture of where I am taking the team and why it is an exciting destination? The story adds richness, provides context, and helps you appreciate what I am trying to build as a leader.

You would likely answer all these questions differently if I responded to your initial inquiry with "We aspire to be the preeminent provider of value-added best-in-class leadership training delivered in high-impact cross-functional environments that leverage all the human capital assets of our clients in a way that drives engagement, empowerment, and synergy across the worldwide enterprise." Yuck. I feel like I need a shower after writing that last one.

There are plenty of great examples of vision statements. A few of my favorites follow.

- *Microsoft:* Create experiences that combine the magic of software with the power of Internet services across a world of devices.
- *Procter & Gamble:* We will provide branded products and services of superior quality and value that improve the lives of the world's consumers.
- *Harley-Davidson:* We fulfill dreams inspired by the many roads of the world by providing extraordinary motorcycles and customer experiences. We fuel the passion for freedom in our customers to express their own individuality.

These vision statements paint a picture of an exciting future in a clear and straightforward way. Anyone who joins the team at Microsoft, P&G, or Harley-Davidson knows where the organization is headed and how they can contribute. They are simple, clear, and lack buzzwords; most important, they inspire teams and help people understand how their contributions and actions drive toward a broader goal. Your own vision statement maxim will obviously be very different, but it needs to achieve these same results.

I once worked with the president of a division who had responsibility for the company's products across all of Europe. The challenge Olaf faced was that his division sold globally recognized branded products but his teams were organized by country. There were large inefficiencies and many redundancies that he wanted to eliminate, but he faced substantial resistance from the country-based teams. Their resistance centered on the idea that each country in Europe was a different market and that serving those different customers required the organization to have country-based capabilities. Getting his country-based teams to adopt the global brand strategies was a key to successful growth for his division.

Olaf articulated his vision for his division simply and crisply when he said "Global brands meeting local needs." He sent a strong message that the global brands came first but that he still saw country-based capabilities as a key to success. Once his teams recognized he was shifting the emphasis to the global brands but that he was not dismantling the entire country-based infrastructure, they were able to direct their energies toward the shift he desired. Over time, the global brand strategies helped him drive growth in many European countries and his division's financial performance improved on a regular basis. His clarity of vision helped him break through organizational resistance and move the division to a better future.

WRITING YOUR MAXIM

It is time to start working on your vision maxim. If your organization already has a vision statement, pull it out and read it carefully. Is it clear what you are trying to become? Is it inspiring? Is it actionable? Is it aspirational? If so, you have it pretty easy. Simply adopt it as your own leadership maxim. If not, you have some work to do.

To create this maxim, look five years into the future and ask yourself what your organization should look like. Using a five-year planning window will generally help you reach a balance: achievable but not too ambitious. This is because it is a short enough time frame for you and your team to have a measurable impact and feel like you have made progress, but it is far enough in the future that you can be aspirational in how you describe that vision without protests of "We'll never achieve that goal in that short an amount of time!" Conversely, vision statements stretching beyond five years into the future can lead your team to feel like the world will change so much over that period that the vision statement will be neither achievable nor relevant. However, your particular situation might call for a longer or shorter time frame depending on the nature of your organization and your industry.

I have provided some thought starters to assist you with tackling this big question. Spend time reflecting on them by yourself and then get your preliminary thoughts down on paper. This is not an exhaustive set of questions nor will every one of them apply to your particular situation. Do your best to answer as many of them as you can, even if at first glance a question does not apply to you. As you consider your own situation, other questions may come to mind. Feel free to include and answer them if doing so will help you articulate a clearer and more compelling vision.

- How big will your organization be? How will you define its scope?
- What new skills will your team members have?
- What new capabilities will you build over this time period?
- How will the way you work with other groups change?
- What should your customers, both internal and external, expect from you?
- What will set your team apart and distinguish it when it is compared to other teams?
- What is your future vision for your team?
- Will they be excited by it?
- What aspects of it will they find inspiring?

Be sure to push the extent of this vision maxim out far enough: beyond where things are clear but not so far that your vision will not be achievable within a reasonable period of time. Once you have drafted a preliminary set of answers to these questions, look at all the answers as pieces of a bigger puzzle. Synthesize the most powerful elements into the simplest statement you can. For example, if you run a home improvement tools product development team, your vision maxim might be "To create new home improvement tools that make the handyman's job safe, easy, and enjoyable." Sure, it's not earth-shattering, but it lets your team know what they are building toward. Write down the statement that encapsulates what your team is all about. That is your first rough draft of a vision maxim. As you evaluate the resulting maxim, ask yourself these questions:

- Is my maxim clear on how my organization creates value?
- Is the maxim ambitious but realistically possible?
- Is the maxim worth pursuing, and will it win people's commitment?
- Does the maxim explain how we differentiate ourselves from competitors?
- Is the maxim concise, consisting of only a few critical words?

How does the first draft of your vision maxim stack up against these questions? If you are not happy with your maxim relative to these questions, continue to revise it until you are.

After you have a maxim you are happy with, schedule one-on-one time with key members of your team. Include people from multiple levels of the organization. Start by sharing the maxim without going into the story behind it. Vision maxims should stand on their own, and though the stories behind them provide richer context, they should not be necessary for the maxim to be understandable. Ask your team for their honest thoughts and opinions. Ideally they are comfortable enough with you and trust you enough to give honest feedback. See what your team members' reactions are and modify the vision maxim accordingly. If they are not clear on some aspects of the maxim or if they are not excited by it, revise it to make it clearer or more exciting. If they think you have missed some things that should be included, consider adding them. Be careful, though! This needs to be *your* vision maxim, so you need to protect it from becoming one created by committee so it doesn't turn into a two-page manifesto. Do not water down the maxim or add extraneous information. This is always a risk when others get involved in crafting a maxim. Incorporate their feedback to the extent that it clarifies your vision maxim or makes it more compelling, then reevaluate it using the preceding questions. Once you and your team are satisfied with the results, document the maxim in Appendix B.

Your team is looking to you to set the course. They want you to not only tell them where you are taking them but also why that is a good place to go. When you write your vision maxim, you are setting that course. The vision you articulate helps put their work into context and lets them see how their efforts contribute to the goals of the broader organization. The clearer and more compelling you can make this vision maxim, the higher the likelihood your team will understand it, support it, and work toward it. It is your vision maxim that will get everyone moving in the same direction with purpose and excitement. Once you have set the direction, your next task is to identify the opportunities you will pursue to get you to your destination.

CHAPTER 12

[HOW WILL YOU FORESEE THE FUTURE?]

Your team looks to you for new ideas, inspiration, and indicators of how you want to approach change. If you personally never challenge the status quo, you cannot expect them to bring you a bevy of new ideas to help you achieve your vision. You must first force yourself to regularly question the way things are, so you can break through the "that's the way we've always done it" barrier to create something new. This kind of questioning will help you identify new opportunities or threats before it is too late to do something about them. Vision is great, but action is what gets you there, and for action to occur, you must first identify the opportunities and ideas on which to act.

CHALLENGING THE STATUS QUO

Many leaders become complacent about looking into the future. They believe they know what lies ahead for their organization. They stop focusing on the future because it seems clear what is in store for them, and they believe that the best use of their energy is to drive current operations. These leaders would do well to heed the sage words of Paul Saffo: "Never mistake a clear view for a short distance." Great leaders consistently look beyond clarity into the uncomfortable ambiguity ahead. They embrace their responsibility to find new ideas that prepare their organization to win in uncertain future environments. Failure to look beyond those short distances will lead you to miss the opportunities and crises that inevitably await.

Do not expect to have all the answers. You will not create all the ideas by yourself. Your team, peers, customers, boss, and other affected stakeholders in your organization will help you identify new opportunities and generate new ideas. Your role in leading the thinking is leading the team to have the right conversation in the first place. Remember, *asking the right questions about the future is more powerful than having the right answers about the past.* To lead the thinking, you must see beyond current probabilities to create future possibilities. A maxim designed to remind you to reconsider the world around you is a fantastic jumping-off point for this kind of thinking.

It is easy to be overcome by daily events, and it can be difficult to carve out the mental space required to reflect on your business amid all the meetings, reports, projects, presentations, emails, and dozens of other tasks that consume our time and energy. Your maxim will serve as a regular reminder to call time-out and ask the important questions everyone else is ignoring. Such dedicated "think time" temporarily erases your mental whiteboard and gives you the room you need to draw up new plans and ideas.

One of the biggest barriers to creating new ideas is the raw inertia of organizations. Personally, I am not satisfied with "the way we've always done it." Whenever I am given an explanation of how the organization does something, I ask "Why?" five times. That's my maxim:

Why? Why? Why? Why? Why?

By the time I get to the fifth why, I have usually found an insight or an opportunity to improve something.

Because my maxim is simply five whys, it serves as a regular reminder for me to challenge the status quo, continue to learn, and seek new opportunities to do things differently. It also helps me ferret out risks to the business if those five whys reveal outdated assumptions about the world. If we are doing something based on old assumptions and the new reality is different, the actions we are taking are potentially wrong, and we could be unwittingly damaging our business. I see it as my responsibility to find and defuse those time bombs before they blow up in our faces.

I am not the creator of the five whys, but I loved it so much the first time I heard it that I adopted it as my maxim. It is more than a concept to me, though. There is a personal and emotional story behind it. I stole the five whys from one of my first consulting engagement managers. He stole it from the leaders who had taught him and so on. I invite you to steal it from me if you like.

Here's what happened. My manager and I were standing in line, grabbing lunch at the client site. I explained some complex data and trends I had analyzed earlier in the day. He asked "Why?" In response, I offered a thought on why those trends were occurring. He asked "Why?" again. I stopped and thought about my explanation of the trends. Again I offered my thoughts on the implications of my prior conclusion. He asked "Why?" a third time.

I snapped. "What the hell, dude?"

He then explained how asking "Why?" enough times can lead you to truly understand an issue and generate meaningful insights. He taught me how one simple question, asked repeatedly, could push me to think beyond where we had already thought. I fell in love with the concept. I learned a lot working with that engagement manager and enjoyed my time with him. For me, it is appropriate to have a maxim based on things he taught me. It has been a maxim of mine ever since. Remember, maxims should have personal meaning for you.

Once I have used the five whys to find an insight, I rely on a second thought leadership maxim to move my thinking forward from insight to action:

So what? So what? So what? So what? So what?
So what? So what?

To use this maxim, I take that insight I found by using the five whys, and I ask "So what?" (up to) seven times. To expand on the "So what?" question, I am really saying *That is my conclusion—so what should we do about it?* Once I have a proposed action, I ask the next "So what?" to move the thinking forward even farther. The expansion of that question is "That is the action I should take. So what should I do next if that action is successful?" With every "So what?" I ask, I push my thinking farther down the path and beyond where I could previously see clearly. Some of my possible actions that come as a result of these inquiries will be wrong, but that's OK. At least I am trying to foresee what I might do, rather than sitting back and reacting to the world as it comes at me. By asking "So what?" repeatedly, I am identifying the implications of an insight to drive an action which drives the next action. Usually by the time I get to the fifth or sixth "So what?" I have identified a new idea to pursue that I had not previously considered.

Using the five whys and the seven so whats, I have found more than my fair share of innovative ideas. I get excited when I think back to when I first learned them from that manager, and that emotion fuels my innovation engine. I use these maxims regularly to lead the thinking, both within my organization and for my clients. These maxims help me look toward the future and generate new opportunities we can pursue. They push me past organizational inertia and create momentum toward my vision. All leaders must challenge the status quo and guide the actions of their organizations toward constantly shifting visions. Leaders who do this well will be the shapers of the market, and other organizations will be the ones reacting to the changing marketplace. It is much better to lead the change than to be led by it.

Here is another example to further demonstrate how repeated simple questions can help you identify and capitalize on new ideas. I worked with one leader who was responsible for managing a network of external partner organizations. There were about a thousand such companies he dealt with on a regular basis. Those organizations all submitted orders and payments to the leader's company throughout the month. As he reviewed his business, he saw some alarming trends. Turnaround times on transactions were getting unacceptably high. Cash flows were slowing down and accounts receivable days outstanding were growing.

He too knew the five whys and the seven so whats. He asked "Why?" several times. He came to learn that many of the transactions were paper-based rather than electronic, because many companies in the partner network found it easier to submit paper than electronic remittances. Why? They had not invested in the payment technology or in training their people how to use it. Why? Because, according to one of the partner CEOs, "We have never had a financial incentive to change to electronic payments." Why? The leader's company and its competitors had never considered changing the process or how they compensated these organizations.

The leader took the next step and began driving action by asking "So what?" several times. He arrived at a plan that changed commissions for the partner organizations based on how many paper payments and orders they sent instead of electronic remittances. In the past, the partners had received full commission regardless of whether they sent in paper or electronic remittances. Under the new plan they received no commission for paper remittances but full commission for electronic ones. The answers to his "So what?" questions uncovered implementation hurdles, technology challenges, and communication issues he would have to overcome.

These questions also helped him appreciate the competitive advantage he could gain by moving first and moving quickly. The partners were submitting paper remittances not only to his company but also to all the leader's competitors. If he forced his partners to shift to electronic remittances the leader would save money on the paper remittances that were still being submitted during the partner companies' electronic platform implementation period. After that implementation period, all the partner companies would be submitting 100-percent electronic remittances. Because the leader was moving in advance of his competitors, he was capturing the savings as the partner companies shifted to electronic remittances. Once his competitors found out about and reacted to the change, there would be little value for them to extract from the market, because the leader would have already captured the vast majority of the gains. If the leader's competitors mandated a change to electronic remittances, the partner companies could do so immediately, because the leader had already forced them onto the electronic platform. Thus his competitors derived no savings from reduced commissions for paper remittances, because the partners had already gone fully electronic.

The five whys and seven so whats helped this leader identify a new opportunity, understand its implications, and take action to drive toward his vision of being the most advanced, efficient, and technology-driven company in the market. These actions also generated large profits for his organization. By the time his competitors made the same change, there was little if any value they could capture.

Sometimes challenging the status quo on a regular basis is simply a matter of looking at your world through a different lens and asking tough questions. When you apply that lens to everything you do, new and interesting opportunities can emerge. That lens and those questions can serve as powerful thought leadership maxims.

WRITING YOUR MAXIMS

Now that you've seen some examples of other maxims in action, let's construct your maxim for identifying new opportunities. You need a maxim that will consistently lead your gaze forward to a place beyond what you can easily see. It must be a thought that gets you to look at all problems differently. It should provide insight on a wide spectrum of changes, from ideas as small as how to change processes to concepts as large as how to redefine your industry. The maxim must force you to step away from the constraints of daily operations and look differently at the world around you.

I want you to create some dedicated think time to consider this one, because this will be one of your more cerebral maxims. As you create your maxim, keep two things in mind. First, it must remind you to think beyond the status quo and challenge the way things are usually done. Second, it should articulate to your team your new approach to thinking in a manner such that they too can identify new opportunities.

Here are a few questions and ideas to get you started on this thinking:

- What is the most innovative or visionary idea you have ever seen?
- What is the best idea you have ever had?
- Has there been a time when you saw an opportunity or a threat before everyone else around you, and you did something about it?
- When you saw that threat or opportunity before others did, was there something specific that led you to look at the situation differently and see things others did not?
- What would it take to get you to step outside your normal way of viewing the world and look at it from a different perspective on a regular basis?
- What do you believe are your biggest limitations to innovation, and how can you remove them?

You know the drill—start writing down the stories, phrases, ideas, and memories that come to mind as you consider these questions. If quotes or passages in this chapter resonate for you, go ahead and write those down too. Get as many ideas down on paper as you can, then step away from your work for a while. When you return to it, look for themes or recurring stories from your past. Synthesize those themes into a pithy statement that reminds you to look into the future on a regular basis. Pick the story you have the strongest emotional connection to and distill it into a simple statement. That statement should cause you to look toward the future for new opportunities or challenges every time you read it and remember the story behind it. This synthesis of themes or the distillation of that story is your maxim for looking to the future and identifying new opportunities. If, for example, you had a leader at one point who always told you "Challenge everything" and in doing so inspired you to find new ideas, then that phrase could be your maxim.

This maxim is designed to force you out of your comfort zone and look at the world differently. Have you written a maxim powerful enough to do that on a consistent basis? Ask yourself these questions:

- Does this maxim help me set aside present constraints that limit my thinking?
- Will this maxim provide a new lens for looking at problems or opportunities I face?
- After reading this maxim, do I find myself considering alternate futures and possibilities?
- Does this maxim lead me to challenge my assumptions and explore new lines of thinking?

If you answered "yes" to these questions, write your maxim down in Appendix B. You have created a maxim that will help you see farther into the future and create new opportunities for your organization. This future view should also help you head off looming crises before they become major problems. If your maxim does not lead you to challenge your thinking and look beyond your present reality, continue refining it until you write one that does.

Leading the thinking and identifying future threats and opportunities requires you to proactively look outside of your daily grind and question your assumptions about the way the world works. Your team is looking to you for insights and ideas, as you should be looking to them for the same. A maxim that permits and encourages new ways of thinking will remind you and your team to regularly make the time for this type of inquiry. If crafted well, this maxim will help you identify and capture opportunities for innovation and prevent potential threats before your competitors are aware of them. Once you have written your maxims for generating new ideas, you need to write a maxim designed to spur you into action.

CHAPTER 13

AFTER ALL THAT THINKING, HOW WILL YOU DRIVE ACTION?

Enough with all the thinking already! Now you need to drive action. Ideas are great, but someone has to set them in motion for them to be worthwhile, and deciding to do that is no easy task. Acting on a decision can be terrifying, especially when it means large-scale change. Your decision may affect a significant number of people, and what if it is the wrong decision? What if things do not go as expected and the resulting outcome negatively affects you or your organization? You could lose your job. Worse, hundreds of other people could lose theirs. It is hard enough to act on decisions when just facing your own insecurities. Throw the complexities of your organization into the mix, and the angst increases exponentially. Politics, lack of resources, uncertainty, doubt, and fear all mess with our minds right when we are on the verge of taking action.

LEADING CHANGE

However, I am challenging you to be thought *leaders*. Being a thought leader requires you to be bold. Your decisions must be clear and forceful. The "thought" part of the equation only gets you halfway to your destination. As my colleague Alan Veeck says, "It's good to have thoughts, but that's not enough." Being a true thought leader means you not only agitate for but also lead change. Such leadership requires decisive action on your part.

You probably see it all the time—people and teams suffering from analysis paralysis. They are unable to make a decision, so instead their organization languishes in the purgatory of endless Excel models. People fear making decisions. They sometimes believe, erroneously for the most part, that they are better off making no decision than making an incorrect one. They think that by not making a decision, they can avoid being fired or disciplined for being wrong. An old maxim of mine that addressed this issue was a lyric from the band Rush, in their song "Freewill":

If you choose not to decide you still have made a choice.

Inaction is still an action. It is choosing not to choose. When decisions are not made, organizations stagnate and eventually go down the tubes. That is when the *really* hard decisions have to be made. Layoffs, restructuring, divestitures, and other painful choices await organizations that cannot make a decision and act on it.

I once worked for a great boss who helped me realize the negative impact of analysis paralysis. I presented a business case to him for a new idea that, based on my analysis, I estimated was worth $1,000,000 in income over the next twelve months. He asked if I was implementing the idea immediately. I told him I was going to do some additional analysis, and then go live the following week with the change I was proposing. He said, "When you come back next week with your additional analysis, the business case had better be worth another $20,000, because that's what seven days costs at a run rate of $1,000,000. Is your analysis worth $20,000?" My answer was no. We went live that day. Inaction has a quantifiable cost.

Leaders have to make choices. Many times those choices are painful. The decisions a leader makes can affect anywhere from dozens to hundreds to thousands to millions of people. Their actions determine whether someone has a job, gets a raise, or moves to a new city. Leaders create businesses—and close them. And in the most extreme cases their actions change the course of industry and therefore the way we live our lives. Sometimes the results of a leader's actions are spectacular. Other times the results are spectacular disasters. Nonetheless, leaders must make decisions and act.

Having a maxim focused on forcing action is powerful. It will move you from analysis to activity. It will help you be decisive. It should reduce your fear and uncertainty and serve as a clear reminder of how to act during uncertain times. One of my favorite decision-making maxims came from the lips of one of the greatest military leaders in history, General George S. Patton III:

In case of doubt, attack!

Besides the fact that I like the quote, the maxim elicits strong emotions for me. When I was in the army I was a tank platoon leader. My first job consisted of the tactical deployment of four M1A1 main battle tanks manned by fifteen dedicated soldiers. I studied General Patton a great deal during both my time at West Point and my initial armor training as a lieutenant. He was effectively the patron saint of armor. I internalized the notion that the worst action you can take on the battlefield is to take no action at all.

During one of my final field training exercises as a platoon leader, I had to employ this maxim. No, I never saw combat during my time in the service. The only fighting I ever did was in a bar. My military field experience consisted only of war games. Our war game scenario required us to charge across a long, open battlefield to find and destroy the opposing force. My tank was the lead tank of the lead platoon of the lead company of the lead battalion in the brigade combat team. We were the true tip of the spear of a four-hundred-vehicle combined arms unit.

As we sped across the battlefield, we approached a set of hills. There were several passes through those hills to choose from. During our planning before the battle, my commander and I decided I would lead us through a specific pass because it provided the safest and fastest route through the hills. As we raced toward the hills, however, I was unable to tell which of the passes was the one we had chosen during our planning session. The terrain rarely looks like the map, especially when you are moving at forty miles per hour, trying not to get shot by the opposing forces.

I was faced with a difficult set of choices. I could have stopped my unit, pulled out my map, and figured out which pass was the correct one. This would have stopped the forward movement of all units behind me. That would leave four hundred vehicles and their crews sitting in the open, subject to enemy fire, but it would give me the time I needed to identify the right pass. That pass would allow us to safely navigate a treacherous choke point. My other choice was to keep rolling at forty miles per hour and take my best guess as to which pass was the correct one. That option would keep the brigade moving and therefore make it harder to target with artillery and direct fire. It also meant I might lead us into the wrong pass, which could be a literal dead end.

In my moment of doubt, I summoned the words of General Patton and chose to attack. "Driver, go left! Take the left pass!" We attacked. We died—quickly. I should have gone right instead. Fortunately, the units behind us saw the unfolding carnage of my unit being destroyed, and they decided to head toward the correct pass. They flooded through it and crushed the opposing forces on the other side.

I had chosen the wrong pass. That was an issue of being "directionally challenged," which was a particular problem of mine. The choice of direction, however, was not the important decision in this situation. The true decision was whether to stop, analyze the map and terrain, and then choose a pass, or to take my best guess as to which pass was the correct one and continue the attack. While my company was dying in the left pass, it felt like I had made the wrong decision on that call as well. But upon reflection, I think my maxim served me well. Had I stopped to analyze the passes, I could have gotten everyone behind me killed as they were sitting in the open, vulnerable to direct and indirect fire. By my choosing to follow the maxim and attack, my unit died, but the rest of the brigade survived and won the battle.

My decision created an outcome that others could observe and analyze. They now knew where the enemy was and which pass they had chosen to defend. They also knew that the pass on the right was likely undefended. Through my actions, I provided my colleagues with important additional data, and they were able to make better decisions based on new information.

I am not saying my choice of the wrong pass was responsible for our winning the battle. Heck, if I had chosen the right pass, perhaps *all* of us would have survived. The bottom line is, I made the best call I could based on my understanding of the situation. Leaders make decisions. Those decisions are not always the correct ones, but they are better than not making a decision at all. Had I abdicated my responsibility to make a decision in that situation, I would have risked the lives of the entire brigade. Better to choose wrong and have a few of us die than not choose at all and invite certain death for everyone.

General Patton's guidance does not only apply in a tank. His advice makes for effective business decision making too. I once worked on a team that was evaluating changing a bonus plan. The new plan was designed to change associate behaviors to better align with new business goals. Several members of the team wanted to do substantial amounts of analysis. Once they had completed it, they wanted to test the new bonus plan for six months. After that testing they proposed doing more analysis, then roll out the new plan across the organization. All told, it would have taken us a year to get something up and running.

I recommended otherwise. During the meeting, I piped in with "I say do it now across the entire organization." *General Patton said to attack, right?* I reasoned that waiting six months for incremental data would cost far more in opportunity cost than doing something less-than-perfect immediately. I also pointed out the decision was not irrevocable. If the new plan didn't work as we hoped, it would not be difficult or cost much to roll it back to the old plan and readjust based on what had been learned during the immediate broad rollout.

My recommendation won the day. The team rolled out the new bonus plan across all locations, and we monitored the results rigorously. There were a few hiccups, but overall the plan was successful. Decisiveness in the face of ambiguity led the team to capture at least six incremental months of value. Had I been wrong, the cost of my error would not have been significant, because the team had the ability to reverse course. We mitigated the risk of being wrong by implementing a rigorous monitoring plan to track key metrics related to the new bonus structure. My maxim helped me overcome the uncertainty and apprehension I faced as we considered the decision.

WRITING YOUR MAXIMS

Let's turn our attention to you. How do you spur yourself onward to action? What is your approach to decision making? Are you aggressive? Do you make "gut" decisions, or do you prefer to gather as much information as possible before making a call? Do you procrastinate? Are there certain types of decisions you find easier to make than others? Are there any types of decisions you hate making? You need to evaluate how you currently make decisions before articulating a maxim designed to focus your decision-making efforts.

Think about an important decision you have made in the recent past. Choose one that had an outcome you are happy with. What has contributed to your sense of satisfaction with that decision? Is it the result? Are you happy with how people were involved in making the decision? Did your decision get positive attention from someone important in your life? Try to break apart the components and figure out why you are happy with the decision, because those reasons are important drivers of your behavior. Write down these feelings and thoughts.

Now think about a decision you have made that had an outcome you are not happy with. Why are you unhappy with it? Did you simply make the wrong call? Was the process of getting to a decision not to your liking? Are you frustrated with how others were or were not involved in making the decision? Again, break these thoughts and emotions apart to identify the drivers of your dissatisfaction with the decision. Write those down too.

Next, I would like you to consider decisions others have made and go through the same exercise. Choose a decision someone else made that had an outcome you are happy with. Were you involved in the decision-making process? Did the resulting decision benefit you from a career, financial, or lifestyle standpoint? Did it result in your being recognized for good performance? Did the decision simplify your life and make your job easier? Understand the feelings and thoughts you have that are linked to your satisfaction with the decision. Write down the answers to these questions as you consider them.

Now pick a decision someone else made whose outcome made you unhappy. What was it about the decision that upset or frustrated you? Were you not consulted before the decision was made? Was it a rash decision? Did the outcome negatively affect your compensation or did it make your job harder? Should the decision have been postponed until better information was available? What about this decision ticked you off? Write down these sources of dissatisfaction.

Lastly, think about (1) a decision you have been putting off and (2) a decision someone else is putting off. What is preventing you from making your decision? What do you think is holding up the other person? Does fear play a role in the delay? What is the root of that fear? Is additional information required before these decisions can be made? What is causing the delay in getting that information? Is the information really required for the decision, or is it an excuse for putting the decision off? What is the cost of being wrong on the decision if those decisions are made right now? What is the likelihood of being wrong? Would it be better to decide now and possibly be wrong or decide later and definitely be right? What is the cost of waiting?

Once you have written down all these thoughts and feelings, step away from them for a few hours and let them stew. Come back and reread them with a fresh set of eyes so you can write your maxim. Consider these questions:

- Do you notice any commonalities between decisions you have made and decisions others have made that you are happy with? If so, what are they?
- Are there similarities between decisions you have made and decisions others have made you are unhappy with? What are they?
- Are there similarities between the decisions being delayed? What are they?
- What themes emerge as you look across all these decisions, and what are your reactions to them?
- Does one of your stories stand out as an example you would hold up as the pinnacle of great decision making?
- Is one of these decisions so bad you would never want to see it happen again?

Choose one of these stories on which to base your maxim. Which story best inspires in you the need for action and good decision making and will keep you from putting things off or getting sucked into analysis paralysis? Remember, your maxim can be based on either behavior you want to emulate or behavior you never want to see again. The maxim needs to remind you of a decision and the circumstances surrounding it so that when you face another decision, thinking about the maxim will guide you in a productive direction. The story behind your maxim should serve as a model for how you regularly want to make decisions—or how you do *not* want to make them, as the case may be. Perhaps you are a runner and you love Nike's products. If their slogan, "Just do it," came to mind during a time you faced a tough decision and that slogan caused you to move forward, then that can be your maxim. As long as the phrase has meaning for you and you can connect it to the emotions associated with the decision, it can be a good maxim.

If you are by nature too hasty or not thoughtful enough in your decision making, choose the story that will remind you to take a more measured approach to the decisions you make. If you procrastinate and are too slow to make decisions, choose the story that reminds you to make a decent decision now versus making a perfect one much later. The maxim has to work for you and you alone. To evaluate the quality of your maxim, answer these questions:

- If I have doubts about making a decision, will this maxim guide my action and move me toward resolution?

- Do I feel strong emotions when I think about the story underlying this maxim?
- Will my team understand my approach to decision making after they hear this maxim and the story behind it?
- Does the maxim help me balance between speed and accuracy in my decision making?

Once you are satisfied with your decision-making leadership maxim, write it down in Appendix B.

In a risk-averse world, the ability to quickly and confidently make a decision can be a differentiator of performance. There is no shortage of data to analyze or opinions to gather, yet at some point those activities do more harm than good. You need to resist the temptation to avoid decisions out of fear or because of a desire for perfect information. Your decision-making maxim should push you forward and help you reach a decision once you have gathered enough information. Your team and your company need you to take action. A maxim focused on driving that action will remind you that at some point you need to make a choice and move forward.

You have now completed your first draft of maxims for how you will lead the thinking for your organization. You now have a way to tell your team where you are headed, how to increase the likelihood of your safely getting there, and how to make decisions along the way. With your direction now set, it's time to start leading your people to your destination.

PART 4

LEADING YOUR PEOPLE

CHAPTER 14

$$\Big[\text{ WHAT IT MEANS TO LEAD YOUR PEOPLE } \Big]$$

Y ou are a leader. Management and leadership are not the same thing. The difference is simple: *you manage things; you lead people.* Admiral Grace Murray Hopper coined this elegant, clear distinction. Yet there is still a lot of confusion on this point, so let's take a closer look at some of the nuances.

THE DIFFERENCES BETWEEN LEADERSHIP AND MANAGEMENT

Leadership and management work hand in hand, but they are fundamentally different concepts.

Management is task-focused. It is short term. It is a series of checklists and to-do's that ensure the work gets done. It is taking actions to hit a budget number or deliver a project on time. Management is how we execute tasks to achieve a specific desired outcome. Said simply, it is the movement of personnel, materiel, and tasks with an exact set of measurable results in mind.

Managing things consumes a large portion of our time at work. It requires forms, reports, meetings, analyses, and documentation. If left unchecked, such tasks will consume every available moment in the day. Sometimes it seems all we do is work on tasks related to managing the organization. When that happens, we can easily mistake management for leadership. The logic underlying that confusion goes like this:

- Fact 1: We are leaders.
- Fact 2: Leadership is the most important thing we do.
- Fact 3: Because we are leaders, we spend our time on only the most important things.
- Fact 4: All our time is spent working on meetings, reports, forms, and analyses.
- Conclusion: Meetings, reports, forms, and analyses must be leadership, because if they are not, we are not spending our time on the most important things.

The flaws in that logic are obvious when those points are presented starkly in black and white. During the workday, however, it is difficult to differentiate between management and leadership because the world is moving at such a dizzying pace. If those things are not leadership, what is?

Leadership is people-focused. It is the words spoken and actions performed that inspire something deep within another person that leads that person to act independently to advance the interests of the team. Leadership is inspiring and influencing people to act in ways they ordinarily would not.

Inspiration is the key to successful leadership. Great leaders have a keen ability to inspire others to tap into their own wellsprings of energy in a way that unleashes their innate potential. For team members to be properly inspired, the leader must help those individuals see how special they are to those around them. Leadership is demonstrating that you put others before yourself and that your primary interest is their best interest. Leading entails articulating a vision of something larger than the individuals involved, helping those involved understand their role in achieving it, and inspiring them to take on seemingly insurmountable challenges because they believe in your vision to the core of their being.

DEFINING YOUR OWN LEADERSHIP STYLE

All leaders approach leadership in different ways and with different styles. More often than not, though, the leadership tools you may encounter are proscriptive methods that tell you how you should interact with your team. Many of those tools suggest leadership behaviors without considering the multitude of leadership styles that different people have. A particular tool that is easy and effective for some leaders to use may be a struggle for other leaders to apply. The failure to account for varieties of leadership and personality styles is why a "one size fits all" type of leadership toolkit can be frustrating and ineffective.

The leadership behaviors derived from the use of the leadership maxims approach will be in alignment with your own personality and style. That alignment enables authenticity on your part. Your maxims will become a clear tool for articulating *your* style of interacting with members of your team. The more clarity you can provide on how you expect to work with others, the more effectively you can deal with the myriad of interactions you will have with the people with whom you work.

The role of leading people can be frustrating and confusing. We have a hard time with difficult conversations regarding bad news, corrective actions, and feedback. We need a support to lean on to help us through those tough situations. Creating maxims for how you want to lead your people helps you manage those difficult situations and conversations. It sets expectations with your team members for how you will treat them. It also gives you a solid foundation for building consistent behaviors and consistent reactions to unpleasant situations. If you have written your maxim well and communicated it clearly to your team, there are no surprises when unpleasant situations arise.

A client of mine, Alain, ran an operations team in Europe. He put a significant amount of effort into making sure his team members knew what to expect from him.

"I tell them they should always know where I'm coming from and what my expectations of them are. I've found when I am predictable in my responses to certain situations, it makes hard conversations easier to have."

Alain explained some of the guidance he gives his team: "I have an expectation that my people place team interests ahead of personal interests. I have worked on teams before where that was not the case, and I hated that environment, so I decided I would never let a team of mine operate that way. I always tell my people 'Team first' and expect that their actions follow that standard. Sometimes they come to me and tell me that they've made a decision or taken an action, and I've asked, 'Team first?' If they respond 'No,' they are not at all surprised when I send them away to go fix what they've done wrong by violating that principle."

By having a clearly articulated expectation for how his people should behave, Alain is able to guide his team members to meet performance standards by asking a two-word question. His simple yet powerful standard sets a clear and positive tone for his team's behavior. Those two words are his maxim.

If your maxims are simple, clear, and well-communicated, your people will be able to accurately predict your reactions to many situations because they will know your standards and buy into them *ahead of an incident*. If you do not share your maxims prior to a lapse in behavior, you will have to explain your standards and someone's failure to meet them, and to justify the fairness of a punishment, all in that moment. That is a much tougher conversation to have than one in which the standards are clear from the outset. Providing transparency and consistency to your team does wonders for making interactions smooth and peaceful.

WHERE TO START

As with all your maxims, you should write these during times of calm and reflection. This will help you create guidelines that will serve you well when the situation gets volatile, and is especially important when dealing with individuals.

To create your leading your people maxims, you need to explore how you want to interact with those individuals. This self-examination requires you to figure out what you want to stand for and what your team should expect from you in every interaction. You must also think about how you will build their skills and capabilities. Yes, that is a lot to think about. It is even harder to articulate. This is where I have seen many leadership philosophies turn into a load of meaningless buzzwords.

You, on the other hand, are striving for clarity. You need simplicity to achieve that. Answering the following straightforward questions can help you define a powerful set of maxims for leading your people.

- What is your natural style?
- How will you remember to treat your team members as individuals?
- How will you stay connected to your team's reality?
- How will you commit to your people's growth?

The maxims you create to describe how you will lead your people will govern your day-to-day interactions with members of your team. In this part of the book, you will articulate aspects of your style that are comfortable and effective for you. You will create maxims to remind you to treat your team members with respect, both for who they are as individuals as well as for the work they do on a daily basis. Finally, you will generate maxims to help you remember to take some risks and give your people opportunities to grow their skills, experiences, and careers. By answering these four questions, you will create a team environment in which people feel comfortable, valued, and challenged. You likely often hear a great deal about how important "employee engagement" is. If you write these maxims well and live them every day, you will have some of the most engaged employees you have ever seen.

You are not automatically a leader by virtue of the box you occupy on an org chart. Leadership is defined by how you relate to the people around you. It is comprised of your personal style, the way you view and treat others, and how you help people become more than they ever thought they could be. It is easy to manage—simply check off the tasks on the to-do list and get them done on time. It is difficult to lead—it requires effort, constant attention, and a selfless approach to your work. If you consistently focus on leading, the managing tends to take care of itself. I encourage you to invest the energy in defining how you will lead your people, because the returns on that effort will come in the form of higher morale, better performance, and a more pleasant and energizing workplace.

CHAPTER 15

[WHAT IS YOUR NATURAL STYLE?]

You probably often hear the "A" word—*authentic*—at your work-place. Authenticity is a simple concept. It is defined as being genuine. Or, in my words, it is a state of being in which what you see is what you get. Expanding that thought to authentic leadership means that the leader is the same person when leading as in any other situation. Authentic leaders' beliefs and values do not change from one scenario to the next. Their reactions to events do not differ depending on who is listening. Their words, perspectives, and opinions are spoken from the heart, and they believe deeply in all of them. An authentic leader does not say what people *want* to hear, but instead says the things people *need* to hear, whether they want to hear them or not. Those same leaders take actions consistent with their thoughts and beliefs. When asked to take action in conflict with their ideals, they take a stand against those actions or at least voice their disapproval and make others convince them it is the right path to pursue. The sum of these genuine words, actions, and beliefs over time defines a leader's style.

Style is a construct through which leaders demonstrate their authenticity. There are many ways to convey ideas, beliefs, and values. There are just as many ways of putting ideas into action. By now you have likely found approaches for communicating and acting that are comfortable for you and other approaches that are not. Those comfortable techniques become your preferred style over time.

FINDING YOUR STYLE

It is important that you know your style, can articulate it clearly, and are comfortable living it every day. To accomplish this, you must find the approaches to communicating and acting that work best for you and then continue to use and hone those techniques so that you maintain your confidence in their efficacy. A virtuous circle will result. The more you use a tool, the better you get at using it and the more inclined you will be to use it. Using tools that allow you to comfortably convey your values and beliefs will eventually form the basis for your natural style. That is the key to being authentic in your leadership.

For me, authenticity stems from how I interact with people. I am a WYSIWYG kind of guy (what you see is what you get). If I think something is fantastic, I say it is fantastic. If I believe something is stupid, I do not hesitate to express my concerns. As I consistently behave in this up-front manner and do not hide my true thoughts, people get to know where I stand on the vast majority of issues. I realize not everyone appreciates this approach. In some cases people downright do not like me because of it. But I would rather have a few people not like me because I express what I truly think than try to curry favor with a few people by being someone I am not.

I have seen the power of authenticity firsthand. One of my clients runs a team of senior-level people from around the globe. She once had to make a series of major organizational changes, and she knew many of them would be painful and difficult for the people who had to execute those changes. Rather than veiling the hard choices in corporate-speak and vague suggestions, she spoke to her team plainly and directly:

"I know you won't agree with all these changes, and I know much of what I'm asking of you is very difficult to do. That said, you are my leadership team, and I need you to execute and support these changes to improve our group's performance."

She then explained each change in a straightforward and simple manner. Although her team members were not thrilled with the changes being made, which included reassignments and some layoffs, they appreciated her candor and expressed their gratitude for the way she approached the conversation. Several of her team members mentioned how her approach increased their trust in her because they felt she had told them everything she knew about the reorganization. Her authenticity helped eliminate doubts in her team members' minds and enabled them to focus on the difficult changes ahead rather than wasting energy trying to decode hidden messages that might have been in her words.

Leadership is not a popularity contest. When I share my thoughts candidly, I remove uncertainty for the people around me. Because I articulate my leadership style to my team and back that up with my words and actions, my reaction in almost any situation will be highly predictable. My views on how I expect people to approach work and team leadership are well-established, and my actions are consistent with those beliefs. After being in leadership roles dating all the way back to my teens, the sum of my experiences, both positive and negative, has shaped how I behave, what I expect of my leaders, and what my team should expect of me. My natural style maxims center on how I will treat and take care of my team and how I expect them to behave. Those maxims are

Kick up. Kiss down.

Don't bring me problems. Bring me solutions.

"Kick up, kiss down" was taught to me by a senior executive. He not only explained the idea—he lived it. The basic premise is that a leader's job is to keep higher-ups mindful of how their decisions affect the leader's people and to give the higher-ups a pointed kick when they have a negative impact on the team. The second part, about kissing down, reminds the leader to praise and encourage the team whenever the opportunity arises. This maxim is obviously the opposite of the "kiss up, kick down" doctrine that can be alarmingly prevalent among managers.

The leader who explained "kick up, kiss down" to me was my boss's boss's boss when I was managing a team of associates. He was an even-keeled guy who rarely, if ever, raised his voice or appeared upset. As I entered his office for a meeting one afternoon, I heard him yelling in the phone and berating the person on the other end of the line. I caught him in the middle of saying " . . . and I can't believe you did that without checking with me first. Do you have any idea how stupid that decision is? I cannot fathom how you missed all the secondary impacts of making that call. Even worse, you never consulted me on it, because if you had, I would have told you *exactly* how stupid a decision you were about to make was I have to go. I have an important meeting now."

I was slightly taken aback, because I had never heard this leader this upset. I sat down and asked with whom he had been speaking.

"It was Kevin."

I knew only one Kevin, and he was this leader's boss.

"He made some idiotic decision, and I'm just now finding out about it. It's going to be a complete pain in the ass for you guys to implement. I'm furious he didn't consult me first, because I could have explained the negative impacts. Sorry you had to listen to me yelling, but 'kick up and kiss down,' you know?"

I asked him to clarify the last part of his reply.

"The way I see it, my job is to give senior leadership a swift kick in the behind when they deserve it. This was one of those times. My responsibility is to take care of you guys and make sure you can get your jobs done effectively and without any interference from silly decisions made in an ivory tower. The kissing down part is all about letting people on my team know they're appreciated and valued. Kick up, kiss down."

Ever since seeing him live that approach, I have held this as one of my personal maxims. I even used it on him once. He recommended that my team take on a new project and shift our priorities. I went into his office, shut the door, and explained how harebrained that decision was. I had made sure to bring facts and additional information to prove my case, and by the end of our conversation, he reversed his recommendation. As I walked out, I said "Kick up, right?" He smiled and nodded.

My second "leadership style" maxim is

Don't bring me problems. Bring me solutions.

I learned this one the hard way. As a young management consultant, I was assigned to a particularly difficult project. Not only was the problem complex, but some members of the client team were not willing to devote sufficient time to making the project succeed. As I walked the halls of our home office one Friday afternoon, one of our senior consulting partners stopped me and asked how things were going. I began unloading a stream of complaints about deadlines, problem complexity, and client team member recalcitrance. The partner listened attentively and allowed me to vent for a few minutes. When I finally paused and caught my breath, he asked, "What's your solution?"

I stared at him blankly. I did not have one.

"Don't bring me problems. Bring me solutions." With that, he walked away.

I was speechless.

When I discussed the interaction with my project manager, she coached me to always have a solution to the problems I bring to others, especially to senior clients or senior consulting partners. She explained that I did not need to have the final answer to solve the entire problem, but I did need to have at least some preliminary suggestions on what steps I thought we should take. In this case, she pointed out, I should have formulated a recommendation that we sit down with the senior client team and discuss the lack of commitment some of their team members were displaying. Having the start of a solution was better than having no solution at all. She made it clear I was not expected to solve all the problems on my own. I was to work with the team to solve them. The point of the whole lesson was that I should try to push a problem as far along as possible on my own before bringing in the team to help. Under no circumstance was I to only bring forth a problem without dedicating any thought to creating a solution, even if that solution was as simple as "We should have a meeting to start figuring this out."

I personally learned a lot and grew a great deal from these particular interactions with the partner and my project manager. I adopted the maxim as my own and have used it with many teams over the years. I am always careful to emphasize that I want my team members to do as much thinking as they can before they come to me with a problem, but they should absolutely come forward once they are stuck and cannot get any closer to a solution. I have found that this maxim empowers my team to make decisions, and it demonstrates that I trust their skill and judgment. It also prevents them from bringing forward small problems they can easily solve on their own. When team members who initially look to me to solve all their problems for them hear this maxim, they respond by either building their own problem-solving skills or moving on to another role in which they can fulfill their need to be spoon-fed. Stylistically the approach works well for me because I enjoy teaching people how to push their thinking and own the results for which they are accountable.

Gabe, a leader of a technology support team, told me how his team members were afraid to take risks because their previous manager always came down hard on them if they ever made a mistake. Their former boss would publicly berate them for even the smallest error. When Gabe took over the team he was swamped with requests they wanted him to approve. "They were coming to me with small decisions they clearly should have made on their own, but they were afraid of making a mistake and being punished. To avoid getting blamed, they simply came to me to let me make the decisions."

Gabe was quickly overwhelmed with all the requests—and frustrated with his team's avoidance of mistakes or risks. He sat the team down and told them, "From now on, I want you to operate with a risk-taking mindset. I want you making your own decisions rather than coming to me for approval. I know you're afraid to make that shift, so I'll make it easy for you—if something goes wrong I want you to think *Blame it on Gabe*. I'll take the fall. I'll accept responsibility if you make a mistake. That's my job as your leader. Just blame it on Gabe if things go wrong."

At first the team hesitantly took small risks to see whether Gabe would live up to his promise. Some people made mistakes, and, true to his word, Gabe took the heat for it. Over time his team came to trust his style of encouraging risk taking, empowering people to make decisions, and taking responsibility for failures when they happened. Gabe found fewer and fewer approval requests crossing his desk, and his team members were much happier and more effective in their jobs because he clearly articulated and lived his personal leadership style.

WRITING YOUR MAXIMS

Now that you have an understanding of what articulating some style maxims looks like, you need to define yours. They must ring true for who you are and how you like to operate. Remember, you are going for authenticity here. The good news is, writing them should be relatively easy. All you have to do is (1) plainly state how you like to work with others and (2) think about a few stories that exemplify that working style. The hard part is ignoring how you think the world around you *wants* you to act and focusing instead on how *you prefer* to act.

Grab a piece of paper and jot down responses and thoughts about the following questions:

- How would your team members describe your leadership style?
- How would your best friends and family members describe it?
- Recall some interactions you've had with team members in which the conversations went poorly. Did you say or do anything that felt unnatural? If so, why was it unnatural? If you could do it over, how would you handle the situation differently?

- Recall some interactions you have had with team members that were comfortable in which you felt you effectively handled the situation. Which aspects of how you behaved were most natural and comfortable? Which aspects were most effective?

- Think about any personality tests you have taken (such as the Myers-Briggs Type Indicator). What do those tests say about your style?

- If new team members asked how you want them to work with you, what would you tell them? If they asked how you plan on working with them, what would you say?

- If you were no longer constrained by your organization's culture and had the choice to utilize any leadership style or techniques you wanted, which ones would you choose?

Take some time to reflect on what you've written down. Do you see any themes emerge as you read your answers to these questions? Are there particular events or sayings that appear in multiple answers? If someone else read your notes, how would they summarize your preferred leadership style? Do any specific stories come to mind when you think about these questions and your interactions that are powerful for you emotionally?

Allow me to offer an example: imagine you had a boss at some point in your career who insisted that everyone on the team "assume positive intent" when dealing with others. Anytime there was a problem between team members, that leader said "Assume positive intent" and it made the problem easier to solve. If you personally found that approach helpful and productive, that phrase could be your maxim. Once you've found something that captures your true leadership style, articulate the essence of it as best you can. Make sure the saying, story, or motto encapsulates the personal aspects of your style.

This is your first draft of your leadership style maxims. Before you record them in Appendix B, do some quality control to ensure the maxims are truly personal leadership style maxims. Ask yourself the following:

- If I shared this encapsulation of my style with someone else, would the story behind that saying give the listener deep insight into who I am as a leader and how I expect to interact with my team?

- Can I look myself in the mirror and state confidently that this maxim represents who I truly am?
- Is this maxim a good predictor of how I will behave in virtually any leadership situation?

Did you answer "yes" to these questions? If not, you need to rethink your maxims. Go back and make the maxims more personal. Set aside notions of what others expect your style to be; simply be your genuine self. As you write, do not let anything constrain your ability to articulate who you really are. Strip out any concepts that feel fake or disingenuous. Be sure the maxims are true to you in your purest form. Once you have something authentic to you, record it in Appendix B.

To recap: your style of interacting with others and how you prefer to lead is uniquely your own. When you live your natural style, you are more comfortable, more authentic, and more effective because you spend your energy on leading instead of focusing on maintaining a façade. When you document and eventually share your style maxims with your team, you make yourself more predictable and your expectations are more clearly known. This enables your team to spend their energy on executing the plan rather than spending time trying to figure out how you are going to behave. Only by eliminating false pretenses can you achieve authenticity. You cannot be an effective leader if you are pretending to be something you are not. It is your authentic style that will enable you to make deeper personal connections with your team members, because they can see the *real* you and you can lead them as individuals.

CHAPTER 16

[HOW WILL YOU REMEMBER TO TREAT YOUR TEAM MEMBERS AS INDIVIDUALS?]

The better you understand your people, the better you will relate to them. First and foremost, you must treat them like individuals. No one wants to be a nameless cog in a big machine. All too often we inadvertently make people feel that way.

You disagree? Stop and think. Have you ever heard or said things like the following?

"She's my analyst."

"Talk to my project manager."

"My VP thinks we should do this."

Where are the faces that go with those statements? How different would the culture of our organizations be if "she," "project manager," and "VP" were replaced or augmented with "Terri," "Jack," or "Kim"? People lose their identities when we refer to them by title alone. They begin to feel interchangeable, one-dimensional, and replaceable. If you still disagree, go home and refer to your spouse directly as "husband" or "wife" or your significant other as "fiancée," "boyfriend," or "girlfriend." That would not go over too well, would it? Referring to someone by position or title alone dehumanizes them. Harkening back to the "manage things, lead people" mantra, I would like to call your attention to the word "people"—not "positions." Leading people requires you to treat and understand them as the unique beings they are. The personal foundation of the relationship between leader and led creates the common ground of trust and respect necessary for a good leadership environment. Leadership without personal understanding is superficial, impersonal, and ineffective.

BUILDING PERSONAL RELATIONSHIPS

It can be difficult getting to know people as individuals. Even if we try to learn more about them, the world conspires to limit our opportunities for meaningful conversations. Schedules are crazy, and there is little to no time for conversation of a personal nature. People change roles often. By the time you start to know them, they are moving on to their next role, so why even bother?

Excuses, excuses. I would argue that spending personal time with your people is much more important than a staff meeting or some other routine work. Go grab lunch. Have coffee together. Talk. I am not telling you to become best friends with your people. I am simply encouraging you to know them as more than "my project manager" or "my admin." When they know you care about them as individuals, they are much more interested in giving you everything they've got, because they begin caring about you too. They want to see you succeed because they genuinely like and understand you as a person. Caring inspires them to give you their best effort.

We all want to be recognized for who we are, not for the role we fill. As we have all been told, there is no "I" in team, but there is a

"ME" in there. People want to be part of something greater than they are, but they want to retain their identity and individuality in the process. Here is a little experiment I would like you to conduct: the next time you see a waitress, a bellman, or anyone else in the service industry who wears a nametag, call them by name as you speak with them. Watch their reaction. In the instant you say their name, you have humanized them. I will bet they are much more interested in fulfilling your request simply because you called them by name. The same dynamic applies to members of your team. If you recognize them as individuals, they will be happier and contribute more to the organization.

I have two maxims that consistently remind me to treat my team members as individuals and to get to know them as people as much as I can. One is a gentle behavioral reminder that keeps me focused on learning about others. The other stems from a powerful story in which I witnessed how a small personal gesture unlocked a great deal of potential in an individual and got that person to contribute more than I ever expected.

The maxims I use to remind me to treat my team members as individuals are

You have two ears and one mouth for a reason.

He drinks 7UP.

The first maxim was taught to me by the partner in charge of a consulting project I was assigned to. He was my boss's boss. We were at dinner with the senior leadership team from a new and important client. This was one of my first consulting projects, and I felt a strong need to impress the client executives. I was still a little insecure in my role and my abilities as a consultant.

As we ate, the clients asked me about my background. When I started telling army stories, they expressed a genuine interest. The more interested they got, the more stories I told. By the time we finished eating they had heard about all my military exploits.

After dinner, the consulting partner running the project asked me how I thought dinner went. I said it was a wonderful meal and the clients seemed like fantastic people. Of course I would think that—they had politely sat there and listened to my life's story. The partner then asked me what I had learned about the client over the course of the meal. I paused and thought hard, but I was unable to come up with anything meaningful as a reply. Then he leveled with me.

"Mike, I'm glad you had a good time at dinner. Here's a little feedback for you, along with something you might find helpful going forward: you have two ears and one mouth for a reason."

My problem was now painfully clear.

He went on, "We're here to help the client get better. The only way we can do that is if we understand them and what's on their minds. If you listen twice as much as you talk, you have a much better chance of understanding them than if you do twice the talking and half the listening."

Ouch. The truth can sting—but learning from it helps the pain go away.

From that day forward the maxim he had offered became one of my maxims. I adopted it as a reminder that to understand people you have to listen to them. The maxim reminds me to ask more questions than I answer. When I find I am suffering from a case of motormouth, I try to use this maxim to get myself to shut up and listen. I will admit I am not always successful. I am a pretty loquacious guy—there is a reason I am a speaker for a living. Given my propensities, this maxim is even more important to me than it would be to someone who is naturally introverted. When I remember to apply this maxim, I find I learn a great deal about people and what is important to them. When they are listened to, they feel valued. My listening tells them I am interested in their stories, backgrounds, problems, and perspectives. In short, they feel like they matter.

My maxim "He drinks 7UP" comes from an interaction I had with one of my junior soldiers when I was a platoon leader. This particular soldier—we'll call him Private Schmedlap—was not a model soldier. He was what we affectionately referred to as a "problem child." He would show up late for work. His uniform was always unkempt. He even showed up drunk at formation one day. He was so drunk the breathalyzer we administered registered a score of "you've got to be kidding." When we went on field exercises, he had to be constantly supervised. If he was not micromanaged, he loafed as much as he could get away with. Despite all my best efforts to get him to change his ways, he seemed determined to be the worst soldier he possibly could be.

We conducted one particular field exercise on an extremely hot day. We were all on a break playing cards in our tent behind the tank gunnery range. I gave my driver five dollars and asked him to run down to the snack tent and buy sodas for everyone. As he prepared to walk out of our tent, I stopped him and gave him a list with everyone's name on it and alongside their name, a brand of soda. "Go get two Pepsis, a Dr. Pepper, three Sprites, two Cokes, and one 7UP," I told him, and he was promptly on his way. When he returned, he handed the sodas out according to the list I had given him. When he gave Schmedlap his 7UP, he looked up at my driver with a puzzled look on his face.

"You know I drink 7UP?" Schmedlap asked.

"No. The lieutenant said to get it for you." My driver pointed to me.

"You know I drink 7UP, sir?" Schmedlap asked me, sounding surprised.

"Yeah. I know a lot of things about you," I replied. I resumed losing at cards without giving the question another thought.

The next day it was like I had a brand new soldier in the platoon. Schmedlap was doing his job without being told and without being hovered over by his sergeant. He had a smile on his face, and his uniform looked reasonably presentable for a change. All his tasks were completed on schedule. He performed all tasks to the prescribed standard and even exceeded the standard on a few. At the end of the work day I thanked him for his efforts.

"Hey Schmedlap, you did a great job today. I appreciate all your hard work. But I have to ask you something. What the hell is going on?"

"What do you mean sir?"

"This kind of work is not what I normally get from you. Why the sudden improvement?"

"Well sir, yesterday when you got me a 7UP, I realized I wasn't some random private in the platoon to you. That's the first time in a long time someone showed me I matter. Thanks for doing that for me. I figure if you care about me then I should probably care about the work I do for you."

One little soda sent a stronger message than I ever could have imagined. It contained validation, caring, and acknowledgment that the recipient mattered as a human being. Now every time I see a can of 7UP, I remember this interaction. That soda reminds me that understanding the simple wants, needs, and preferences of members of my team goes a long way toward showing them they matter to me as the unique individuals they are. No, I do not always live up to this self-defined standard. It is easy to forget to treat people like important individuals when faced with the pressures of running the operations every day. But I remember to do so more frequently than I might do otherwise if I did not have this maxim.

An executive from an Irish pharmaceutical firm had a different approach to this maxim. Ann told me her maxim is "Be nosy." She explained how early in her career she often felt awkward having conversations with her team members about their personal lives. Derek, a member of Ann's team, started demonstrating poor performance. Ann tried to help him improve, but nothing seemed to work. All the solutions she offered focused on Derek's behavior at the office. Ann tried things like sending him to training, getting him a mentor, and changing his responsibilities. She eventually learned that Derek was having some family issues and those were distracting him from his responsibilities at the office. Once Ann learned of this, she made his role more flexible in terms of working hours so he could address the challenges he faced at home. This increased flexibility did not solve everything, but the situation improved dramatically.

Ann was disappointed in herself for not knowing more about Derek as a person, and she attributed her avoidance of discussing personal issues to her upbringing. "When I was growing up, my mother always told me 'Don't be nosy' whenever I asked someone a personal question. It turns out her advice isn't always correct, so now I remind myself that it's okay to be nosy, because by doing so I can do a better job of taking care of the people on my team. That's my maxim: 'Be nosy.'"

WRITING YOUR MAXIMS

The vast majority of us are well-intentioned, but life can get in the way. It is one thing to express an empty platitude to treat people as individuals. It is another thing entirely to have a regular reminder in front of you that emphasizes the importance of treating people that way every day. That is what a well-articulated maxim can do for you.

Take a moment and write down the names of your direct reports or of people you are responsible for leading on a regular basis. Leave plenty of room on the page under each of their names. Now for each person, write down as many personal things you can think of about that individual. Do not include things like their job description or their current project responsibilities. Focus on capturing things that make them unique. If you are having trouble getting started, try answering these questions:

- Where did they grow up?
- Are they from a big family or a small one?
- Do they have children? Pets? What are their names?
- What are their kids into? Sports? Performing arts?
- What is this person's favorite pastime? Is he a sports fan? Who is his favorite team?
- Does he have any hobbies?
- What is her proudest accomplishment? Her biggest disappointment? Her career aspiration?

Use these questions to guide you, but write down anything else that springs to mind.

Is this an easy exercise for you or is it hard? If your page remains stubbornly barren, you clearly have some work to do getting to know your people better. I am not encouraging you to go beyond the reasonable or appropriate in understanding their personal lives. Yes, you should respect the wishes of those who want to keep their personal lives private, but that is no excuse for not knowing anything about your people if they are willing to share it.

As you conduct this reflection, think of any particular stories or events that exemplify the importance of knowing people as individuals, as my 7UP story does for me. Also, as you write these things down, think about the circumstances surrounding the situations in which you learned the information. Is there any one thing that stands out in your mind that could suitably serve you as a maxim?

If no stories or maxims are leaping off the page for you as you reflect on your team, try reflecting on your relationship with your leaders instead. Think of any situations in which one of your leaders demonstrated they knew and valued you as an individual. Answer the following questions about those situations:

- Who was that leader and what were the circumstances surrounding the interaction?
- How did you feel when that leader demonstrated he or she knew you well and cared about you as an individual?
- How did you perform after you understood and appreciated how the leader viewed you?
- Is there a phrase, image, or event that exemplifies the dynamic between you and that leader?
- When you think of that phrase, image, or event, do you feel those same great feelings you felt when the interaction first occurred?

Regardless of whether the reminder you chose is related to an interaction with a leader or someone on your team, or if you chose one of each, that pointed reminder of your relationship is your maxim. If you are a huge Cleveland Indians fan and one day your boss gave you tickets to an Indians game for your April 6 birthday, your maxim might be something like "Indians versus Red Sox, April 6" because it reminds you of how great it felt when your boss treated you like an individual. Make sure the maxims you choose generate an emotional reaction for you. The emotional surge you feel when you think of these reminders is the key to creating powerful maxims that will change your behaviors and reinforce your new approach to interacting with your people. Without that tug on your gut or your heart, the maxim is doomed to the fate of being an irrelevant platitude. Assess your draft maxim against the following questions to determine whether it is a strong reminder to treat your people as individuals:

- Will this maxim get me to stop thinking of people according to their title and instead get me to think of them as individuals?
- Does this maxim prompt me to learn more about the lives my team members lead outside the workplace?
- Will my people know I care about them as individuals if I regularly live by this maxim?

Affirmative answers to these questions mean you have a solid start on a maxim for treating your people as individuals. If the draft maxim you have written does not change the way you view and interact with your people, consider revising it until it does. Remember, however, that you will continue to revise these maxims over time. Do not overinvest in perfecting them at this stage of the process. Once you have identified the one or two draft maxims that remind you to treat your people as individuals, record them in Appendix B.

By developing your own powerful maxim to serve as a constant reminder to step outside your daily routine and spend time getting to know your people better, you'll now be more likely to actually do so. You will gain a better sense of who they are, what is important to them, and what they are capable of. You will understand what motivates them and what has the opposite effect, and demonstrate that you value them as the unique individuals they are. The more important they know they are to you, the more important you become to them. Eventually that dynamic forms a solid base of respect and loyalty from which you can more effectively lead your people.

CHAPTER 17

[HOW WILL YOU STAY CONNECTED TO YOUR TEAM'S REALITY?]

When I was in the army, we used to follow a leadership principle that stated "Employ your unit in accordance with its capabilities." That principle was important, because you did not want to make the mistake of sending five soldiers carrying rifles out on the battlefield to defeat twenty tanks. Translating this principle to the civilian world, you do not want to ask your people to perform work of which they are incapable. Doing so can frustrate them and leave them demoralized when they fail at the assigned task. The only way you can truly appreciate what your team is or is not capable of is to see it firsthand or, better yet, do it yourself. When you understand what your people do on a daily basis, you know how much you can reasonably ask of them. That knowledge of their work also enhances your credibility and their respect for you.

Have you ever had this experience? Your boss or someone else senior to you asked you to do something that you knew, given the realities of your business and your organization, was impossible? It's frustrating, isn't it? *If he only had a clue* is likely one of the first thoughts that crosses your mind in that situation. You probably elaborate on the stupidity of the request with thoughts like *I can't believe he asked for that. We will never be able to get that done in the time he has given us. Doesn't he know anything about what we go through?*

I will bet you a dime to a dollar your team has said the same thing about you on more than one occasion. I know my teams have said that about me at times. This asking for the impossible is clearly dysfunctional behavior, so why does it happen so often? It happens because we get so caught up in our own worlds and problems that we don't pay enough attention to the challenges our team members face. This lack of attention creates the disconnect. If you ignore your team's reality too often, you will earn a reputation for living in an ivory tower and considering yourself "too good" to associate with the common man. You will be perceived as being above the work you ask your people to do every day and out of touch with the day-to-day operations of the business. Those disconnects erode credibility and respect for you as a leader.

UNDERSTANDING WHAT YOUR PEOPLE DO

If you want to get respect, get dirty. Roll up your sleeves and do the job you are asking your team to do. You obviously can't do this all the time, and depending on what your people do, you might find yourself doing it more or less frequently. When I led call center teams, I would sit in and listen to customer calls or even handle calls myself every couple of months. When I was a platoon leader and I worked closely with my soldiers, I found myself doing "soldierly" tasks every day. Regardless of your position, you should perform tasks that your teams perform frequently enough to get a good understanding of their jobs and often enough that your people realize you take their lives seriously.

There are several reasons to dedicate the time and energy to these efforts. First of all, you will better understand what your people go through on a daily basis. Second, you will be signaling to them you are not above any work you are asking them to do. Most important, the better you understand the tasks they routinely perform, the higher the likelihood that you will ask them to take on only tasks or projects that are possible and reasonable.

To ensure that you demonstrate this behavior regularly, you need to create a maxim that is a reminder to get out there and get dirty.

My reminder to get dirty and stay in touch with what people are doing is rooted in a story of a time when I literally got dirty. It reminds me about the time I crawled under one of my tanks to perform maintenance on it. The maxim is

He's under the tank, sir.

What follows is the story behind it.

My platoon was in the field on training exercises for a couple of weeks. One morning, one of the senior officers in my battalion came to my unit's area to see how things were going. This officer was an "officer's officer," not a "soldier's officer" (a difference that I will explain shortly). He sauntered up to my eighteen-year-old driver, who was a brand new buck private—the lowest-ranking man in the Army. My driver was leaning against our tank taking a break and enjoying a cigarette. As the officer approached, my driver put out his smoke and stood at attention. The officer asked "Where's Lieutenant Figliuolo?"

My driver pointed toward our tank. A pair of boots was sticking out from underneath the vehicle. The officer became irked; clearly my driver was not listening to him. "No. Maybe you didn't understand my question, private. Where is *Lieutenant* Figliuolo?"

"He's under the tank, sir."

"Excuse me?" The officer was profoundly confused.

"I said he's under the tank, sir."

The senior officer bent over and barked "Lieutenant Figliuolo!"

I was so startled by his call that I smacked my head on the underside of the tank. Luckily I was wearing my helmet at the time. I quickly scrambled out from under the vehicle and stood at attention before my superior.

"What are you doing under that tank?" he asked.

"I'm fixing the track, sir."

The officer's eyes widened. "Why are you fixing the track?"

"Because it's broken, and I'm already done with all my other responsibilities, sir."

He shook his head, somewhat befuddled that an officer would be turning a wrench. In his world, vehicle maintenance was the bailiwick of buck privates. Officers were supposed to write operations orders, discipline soldiers, and read maps. My presence under the vehicle gave him a sudden, severe case of cognitive dissonance. It simply did not make sense to him that I was performing maintenance on my vehicle, especially when my driver was standing around enjoying a cigarette.

The senior officer left me with a brusque "Carry on." I don't think he ever figured out what happened that day. The reason my driver was having a smoke break was because he had been up since 2:00 A.M. working on the track, and he was exhausted. I had offered take over repairs while he got some rest.

Needless to say, by lunchtime the story of my exploits under a tank had circulated among all the enlisted men in the company, and by dinnertime the entire battalion knew. Suddenly I was a minor celebrity in the eyes of the soldiers. I was "one of them"—a regular working guy who happened to have an officer's bars on my shoulders. The simple act of crawling in the mud to turn a wrench earned me respect for who I was rather than respect for what I wore on my uniform. It made me a "soldier's officer"—an officer who truly cared about and looked out for his soldiers first and foremost, versus an "officer's officer," more concerned with spit shine and appearances of authority.

I can still hear my driver saying "He's under the tank, sir." It is a simple maxim that reminds me to understand and appreciate my team's reality. The story behind the maxim holds strong emotions for me, and I cannot help but smile when I remember it. When I share the maxim with my team, it lets them know I am not above any work I have the skills to perform, and I am definitely not above doing anything I ask

them to do. The maxim is a perfect way for me to stay in touch with
the work my organization does and the challenges my people face.

I have been on the other end of this cluelessness spectrum, as both
the led and the leader. Two situations stand out for me specifically. In
one, my project leader was clueless; in another, I was the offender.
In the first situation, the partner leading a consulting project to which
I was assigned asked me to build a model to predict certain industry
dynamics. I set about the task eagerly because it was an interesting
problem to solve. The more I worked on the model, the more complex
yet insightful it became. The cluelessness began when the partner
checked in with me to get a status update on my progress. I showed
him the three scenarios I had constructed in the model. Each scenario
was a 5×5 matrix of possible financial outcomes resulting from changing industry dynamics. I explained the matrices and showed him the
results of the first one I had completed. I told him I still needed to
complete the other two matrices.

He asked "How long is it going to take?" as he studied the matrix
in front of him. If you have ever worked on an Excel spreadsheet, it is
pretty easy to tell how simple or complex something is with but a glance.
This model screamed complexity. I told him each box in the matrices
would take about ten minutes to program because of all the variables
involved.

"You're saying you'll have both matrices done in twenty minutes,
then? That's fantastic. Let me know when you're done and we can
discuss the results."

I quickly corrected him. "Um, no. Each *box* in the matrix takes ten
minutes. Each matrix will take about four hours to program. This won't
be ready until tomorrow."

He blinked in disbelief. "There is no way it takes four hours to
model something. You must be doing something wrong, Mike. Let me
see that thing and show me how you program a box in the matrix."

I walked him through the creation of the multiple formulas that
generated one cell in the matrix. After ten minutes of coding he said,

"Oh. Okay. I'll leave you alone now." Throughout my conversation with the partner, my colleagues in the room, who could overhear the whole exchange, giggled in the corner. That partner did not score high marks with us "soldiers" in terms of being in touch with the work his teams did for him. His detachment from the day-to-day hurt his credibility and his reputation. Perhaps if he had had a maxim that reminded him to stay grounded he could have avoided that embarrassing conversation.

This is not to say that any maxim can ensure that you will never again be clueless. Even though I have my "He's under the tank" maxim, I too have been guilty of being completely out of touch with my team's reality. Later in my career, I behaved exactly like the consulting partner. I had taken on a new role managing an organization that tested and launched new consumer-based strategies designed to improve our profitability. Early in my tenure leading the team, I asked them to run a test on a hypothesis I had. I expected the test to be done in a few days, and I made my expectation broadly known. I even told my boss I would have some interesting test results for him in the near future. After hearing me make some of my public proclamations, my team explained to me it would take at least six months for us to run the test and get the results.

I was shocked. Much like the partner who was confused about my Excel model, I thought the team was doing something wrong, and I was not shy about sharing my opinion with them. Unfortunately for me, they were right. They patiently explained all the dynamics of the testing and measurement process until I understood why it was going to take six months. I was a fool for not understanding these challenges, and I was a bigger fool for mouthing off about how quickly we would be done when I lacked a fully grounded perspective on the complexities of the process. I never made that mistake again. Even though I had a compelling and clear maxim designed to keep me grounded in the team's reality, I still made the mistake of letting myself get out of touch with the everyday challenges they dealt with.

It is not enough to have good maxims. You have to use them on a regular basis, too.

WRITING YOUR MAXIMS

To help you avoid the fate of the clueless fool, you need to create maxims for staying in touch with your team's reality. This reality consists of not only the tasks they perform but also the environment in which they perform them. You are lucky. You operate above the fray. Typically, when you ask people to do things, those things get done. After all, you are the boss.

Many of your team members are not that lucky. They deal with organizational roadblocks, politics, and credibility challenges you hopefully overcame years ago. Yes, you have your own set of challenges, and I know *your* boss does not appreciate what *you* go through every day either, but this is not about you. It is about how you lead your team. You need to create a maxim to consistently remind you to get in touch with your team's reality and see the context in which the tasks you are asking them to do must get done. If you understand and appreciate those challenges they face, you can make more reasonable and intelligent requests of them. They will also appreciate and respect you for being cognizant of what they must overcome to achieve the goals you set for them.

To create these maxims, let's start by getting an understanding of what you know about your team members' jobs. Get out a piece of paper and take notes on the following questions:

- What are the major deliverables your team members believe are their highest priority?
- Which activities consume significant amounts of the team's time yet return little in the way of results?
- What are the top obstacles your team faces in getting things done (for example, resource constraints, other groups blocking their efforts, too many priorities, not enough time, lack of clarity on what they need to do)?
- Which difficult aspects of their jobs would your team members say you appreciate the least?
- What subjects would they say you should know a great deal more about?

Once you have cataloged your lack of knowledge and understanding about what your team goes through every day, you need to do something terrifying—go speak with trusted members of your team and validate your responses to these questions. I never said writing your leadership maxims was going to be easy! First, set the context for the conversation by saying something like "I would like to do a better job of helping the team accomplish its goals. I want to get a better understanding of the challenges you face every day so I can ensure the requests I make are reasonable and achievable. I have taken a cut at my understanding of what you go through. I would like to validate that perspective and make it more accurate."

Do not be shocked if your team members jump at the chance to explain their world to you. When they do, remember you have two ears and one mouth for a reason. At first it will be a gripe session, but once they have finished venting you will find the conversation to be productive and informative.

After you have rounded out your understanding of their world, review your notes and answer the following questions:

- Did you identify any themes or major disconnects during this introspection and interview process?
- Do one or two stories that exemplify how you do or do not understand their world show up several times in your notes?
- Were your team members pleasantly surprised that you understood some aspect of their plight in great detail?
- Are there situations from your past when you understood your team's jobs and the result of demonstrating that knowledge was strongly positive?
- Are there situations in which you did not understand their jobs and the result of your lack of knowledge was painful?
- Have you been in situations in which your leader demonstrated that he or she knew your job and could do it as well as, if not better, than you?
- Have you experienced a feeling that your leader had no idea what your job entailed and that lack of knowledge made your work difficult?
- Do any of the observations you have made or the stories you have recalled generate powerful positive or negative feelings within you?

Ideally, as you answer this set of questions, a maxim will begin to emerge. Remember, it can be a story, a phrase, a quote, or an image that reminds you how important it is for you to understand and stay connected to the world your team members live in. Your maxim might come from your experiences with your current team or from a situation in your past. Regardless of whether your maxim is based on your current team or not, you should definitely have the conversation with your team that I just described. The simple act of discussing your team members' challenges with them will build understanding, rapport, and respect, whether those conversations result in being the basis for a maxim or not.

Again, focus on the story that creates the strongest emotional reaction for you and seek to derive your maxim from it. Simplify the maxim by choosing the phrase, image, or other powerful element of the story that will quickly remind you of that event and help you focus your behavior in your desired direction. If, for example, you had a leader who worked side by side with other members of the team during a crunched time frame during budget season, your maxim could be "Karen did the budget." The notion of your leader rolling up her sleeves and pitching in can remind you of how you want to behave during similar situations. That resonant concept is your maxim. Write yours down, take some time away from it, and come back to it after you have reflected on it for a while.

Now that you have written that draft maxim and have had time to think about it, it's time to test it. How well will your draft maxim keep you in touch with your team's reality? Answer the following questions:

- Will this maxim help keep my requests of my team balanced between aggressive and realistic?
- Does this maxim encourage me to learn about the work my team members do and the challenges they face in doing it?
- If I adhere to this maxim, will I always have a solid understanding of the world in which my team members work and live?
- Will my team members know I understand and appreciate the challenges they face?

You should be able to answer each question with an emphatic "yes." If that is the case, you have constructed a strong maxim. If not, keep refining your maxim until you achieve that standard. Once you're satisfied with it, record it in Appendix B. This is your maxim for staying in touch with your team's reality.

Knowing what your team does and what challenges they face is a fundamental aspect of getting the best work out of them. The better you understand the skill and effort required to perform their jobs the more effectively you can coach your people, develop them, and allocate tasks among them. A maxim that keeps you connected to your team's reality helps you avoid earning the reputation of a clueless fool. If your team knows you are well-versed in what they do and that you are not above doing it yourself, your credibility and respect will be enhanced, thereby improving your ability to influence and lead others.

CHAPTER 18

[HOW WILL YOU COMMIT TO YOUR PEOPLE'S GROWTH?]

Your people do not go to work just for the money. They don't show up because they cannot wait to see their boss. They go to work because they want to be challenged. They get excited about growth opportunities. They are driven by a need to be more than they currently are. If you don't believe me, go back and review the section on leading yourself. Why do *you* go to work every day?

Most every one of us would like to go to a job in which we are challenged and have opportunities for growth. Your job as a leader is to create an environment for your team in which that is possible. However, creating this environment can be difficult. Our focus is taken up by the daily chaos of deadlines, projects, and other crises.

Another reason we do not challenge and develop our team is a bit more insidious: fear. We are afraid of losing control. We are afraid of failure. We believe that failure means someone on our team did something wrong, which, in turn, means we as leaders did something wrong. But in order to grow, people need the opportunity to tackle new challenges and overcome new obstacles. This means that sometimes they will fail. I would submit that, under the right conditions, when a member of your team fails at something, you have done something *right* as a leader. You should be taking those calculated risks designed to stretch your people beyond their current skills.

DO NOT BE AFRAID TO CHALLENGE YOUR TEAM

If all you ever assign to the people on your team are tasks they have already mastered, there is not much growth potential for them to take advantage of. And if you are only handing out those simple assignments, you are most likely both frustrating and boring your team members. They have already demonstrated mastery of those tasks. Asking them to do the same task over and over tells them you are not confident in their ability to do more complex or difficult work. I know that is not the message you intend to send. You are assigning the work because they are good at it, and you are confident they will deliver the desired results. But your intent does not matter here. The *perception* of why you are giving them these tasks is what matters. More often than not, people will perceive the negative reasons behind why something is happening rather than looking for the possible positives behind it.

The only way you can really help your people grow is to assign them tasks they are *not yet* capable of. Doing so means you are creating the possibility they might fail. In fact, realistically, they *will* fail—sometimes. But it is also a powerful way to help grow their careers and keep them interested and engaged. In cases when you hesitate to create those opportunities, a maxim can come to your rescue. You need to write a maxim that helps you remember to challenge and develop your people.

My maxim to remind myself to challenge and develop my team is

But he's never done that job!

When I was responsible for the infrastructure support for the operating division of one company where I worked, I had a great person on my team whom I'll refer to as Carson. He was a star analyst, but he had always been an individual contributor. As our organization grew and changed, I needed someone to build a team in his area of responsibility. I had two choices—either hire a proven team builder from outside our organization or take a chance on Carson, knowing he had never managed people before. I told my boss I was going to do the latter.

My boss freaked out a bit. He said, "But he's never done that job! He's never managed people or vendors. Why not bring Terri over from marketing and have her take over the role? She has built at least ten teams that I know of."

I responded with a perspective that became the basis for my maxim. "I know Terri is great, but how excited do you think she will be about doing this for the eleventh time? Besides, someone took a chance on her the first time, right? The way I see it, I am taking the same chance on Carson. He has to learn how to manage people at some point. I'll be there to hold his hand. I've led people before and will coach him on how to lead effectively. I have managed vendors, so I'll show him how to manage them as well. When you think about it, the only drawback here is that I'll have to spend some extra time coaching him. The business will be fine."

"Okay, I guess. It's your team."

Was I taking a chance? Sure. For people to grow, you have to take the chance that they will fail along the way. But Carson already knew the business, my expectations, and my working style. I was not breaking in another "new guy," which can indeed be a significant time sink. Carson was a known quantity to me; therefore my risk of a bad hire was zero. Anyone who has ever made a bad hire knows how damaging that kind of error can be. My rule of thumb is if the person can already do 60 to 80 percent of what is required in the new role, and I can cover 10 to 20 percent of the gap myself through either coaching or surrounding the person with other good people, I take the chance and put them in the role. Over time, the person will grow into the 20 to 40 percent of the job they need to learn and become a much more valuable and happier team member. An ancillary benefit of this approach is that I also build bench strength for the organization. If I had given the role to Terri and she then left for another job, replacing her would have been quite difficult. By taking the chance on Carson, I reduced the risk of talent loss by diversifying the capabilities of people in the organization.

Carson gave it his all. He learned a lot, much of it the hard way—by making mistakes. Over time he ran a great team and did a wonderful job of managing our vendors. I promoted him six months after he took the job. There were plenty of benefits resulting from this move. Carson was happy and loyal to the organization. The team made a lot more money for the company. Word got around that I was willing to take chances on people and help them grow via exciting "stretch" opportunities. Recruiting for open roles was easy for me. My maxim "But he's never done that job!" reminds me of Carson's story. It reinforces the fact that I have to take risks on people and create opportunities for them to develop and grow. When I share this maxim and story with new people on my team, it gives them a clear understanding of my commitment to people development. It also gives them a tool for holding me accountable for creating such opportunities. Any time I get risk-averse and shy away from putting someone in a stretch role, members of my team can help me correct my behavior simply by pointing to this maxim.

The other component of the development equation is feedback. If you are committing to a team member's growth, you first have to give them the opportunity and then ensure that they do, in fact, grow. The only way they will learn and develop in those roles is with coaching and feedback. Giving feedback can be challenging. Many times we nail the easy feedback when we say things like "Great job on beating your goal by 37 percent!" That is not a particularly hard message to deliver. Such feedback is not particularly useful, either. There is no action being requested of the recipient. Your job as the leader is to provide an observation on the recipient's actions *and* give them ideas on what they might do better or differently going forward. That is easy to do in a goal-beating situation, but what about more difficult conversations? Many of us avoid having them because they are uncomfortable, but when you ignore the problem it festers until those conversations turn into very difficult conversations, then extremely difficult conversations, and eventually the "Here's your severance check and pink slip" conversations. I know my first gut instinct is to avoid those early-intervention discussions, but I also know it is my responsibility to have that feedback conversation as soon as possible. I have adopted a maxim designed to hold me accountable for doing exactly that:

> It's easier to correct course 100 yards into the
> journey than 100 miles into it.

The maxim sounds good when you first hear it, and it makes sense on its face, but that is not enough. A maxim must trigger a visceral emotional reaction for it to be effective. My story behind this maxim is about a time I mismanaged a member of my team. Let's call him Bob. He was a well-intentioned and seemingly hard-working guy. Over time, I began to hear feedback from members of his team that he could be rude, abrupt, and demeaning. I would tell the person providing the feedback "Thank you for sharing that with me." And then I would do nothing about it. I had a good relationship with Bob and I rationalized away the complaints. I avoided a mildly uncomfortable conversation.

A few months later Bob did some analysis for me and the results seemed a bit odd. His numbers did not jibe with what I thought was going on in his organization. He explained away some of the variances and errors. His explanations sounded like good reasons on their face, but after giving them some careful thought I realized that those reasons did not make sense. But I let it go, rationalizing that it was not a big deal because in the grand scheme of things Bob was doing an OK job. I was avoiding a difficult conversation.

Several weeks later I stopped by Bob's office to ask him about another nonsensical set of numbers he had submitted. As I approached his office, I heard him yelling at one of his subordinates. It was impossible not to hear him berating this person. The tone and words he used during the screaming bout were harsh and unprofessional. I walked away from his office and told myself I would discuss the incident with him once he calmed down. I never brought it up in our next conversation because it did not seem like the "right time" to do so. I was ducking an extremely uncomfortable conversation.

The next month Bob came to me and told me he had a great opportunity at a new company and he was going to take the job. My first reaction was "Oh no! I'm losing a key member of the team, and it will be hard to fill his role and get all his work done while I look for a replacement." My next reaction was "Whew! He's leaving, which means I don't have to have that awkward year-end review conversation with him."

He took the new job, and everyone was happy. But not really. Upon reflection, I was quite disappointed in my spinelessness during those months. I avoided a simple conversation in which I could have established a performance standard. I ducked increasingly difficult discussions, and I subjected members of his team to mistreatment. Ultimately, my avoidance of the issue put the business at risk. From a personal standpoint, I damaged my reputation and efficacy as a leader. If his team members could not trust me to stand up for them after they came to me with complaints, who could they trust? My behavior created morale issues and sent the wrong message to my people.

On my way home a few evenings later, I called a good friend of mine to have a chat. I told him about Bob's taking the new role; I also told him how disappointed I was in my failure to fix the situation much earlier in the year. My friend listened attentively to the story, and when I finished he said, "Remember, it's easier to correct course 100 yards into the journey than 100 miles into it."

This was the swift smack upside the head that I needed. His words stuck with me, and I adopted them as a maxim I still use to this day. Since that conversation there have been multiple occasions when I have had to deliver some uncomfortable messages. When that nagging avoidance instinct crops up, I remember this maxim and deliver the required feedback in a direct, constructive, and timely manner. I have not had a single "extremely difficult" conversation since I adopted this maxim. The emotional nature of the maxim and my visceral reaction to it spur me to action. The actions I then take are the behavior changes required to make the maxim effective. The positive results of those actions reinforce my use of the maxim, and the virtuous circle grows.

You should regularly be looking for opportunities to challenge people on your team by putting them in situations in which they can learn and grow. Providing feedback and coaching is an integral part of helping with that growth. You should also always look for opportunities to give feedback, regardless of whether or not it entails taking on new challenges. I do not think I need to expound the importance of these points. But I do need to emphasize the importance of doing these things on a consistent basis and not letting them fall by the wayside simply because they are hard. The frenzy of daily operations commands your attention. Without a maxim to remind you to fulfill these other leadership responsibilities, you run the risk of not doing these things at all. When that happens, you suffer, your team suffers, and your organization suffers.

WRITING YOUR MAXIMS

Think about a situation or experience in which you were challenged every day. Choose a situation that forced your skills to grow more than any other time in your career. Reflect upon how many times since then you have used the skills you learned in that situation. Consider how the growth you experienced during that time has advanced your career and gotten you where you are today. Recognizing that growth feels pretty good, doesn't it? Even if the situation you are thinking of was painful and difficult at the time, the intervening passage of time has most likely enabled you to put the pain in perspective and recognize the benefits of having overcome any challenges associated with those incidents. Write down some of the key elements of this situation. Capture some phrases, quotes, or pointed reminders of the situation that bring back all these memories.

Now consider a time when you were bored with your work. Think about the drudgery of performing tasks you could do in your sleep.

Remember the frustration you felt when you thought your manager did not believe you were capable of more challenging work. Did you do your best work in these circumstances? Would you consider yourself "engaged" during those times? Did you truly feel like you earned what you were being paid while you were being underutilized? Write down the thoughts and feelings that surface when you reflect on your time in Boringville. Are there emotional triggers associated with this painful period? Do you remember anything that causes a flood of memories and emotions related to this situation to rush to the fore? Add these feelings, thoughts, quotes, and triggers to the list of things you have already written down.

Next, I want you to reflect on times you have either failed or been wildly successful. Those times can range from work scenarios to sports to personal projects. Choose experiences that involved someone else coaching you and helping you learn from those successes and failures. Write down what you learned and how that person inspired and coached you. What new skills did you acquire from this experience? How are you a better person because of the way this coach or mentor was involved in the aftermath of your failure or during the glow of your success?

Once you have captured your own experiences of being challenged, bored, failing, and succeeding, think about your time as a leader. Have any of your team members had these experiences? Recall any situations in which you challenged a member of your team and helped that person grow. Also think about any situations in which someone who worked for you was bored and uninspired. Remember some of your team members' failures and how you coached them to do better next time. Consider their successes and the role you played in helping them achieve these. Capture those memories in the form of emotional triggers, sayings, or other simple encapsulations of those incidents.

After you have completed the evaluation of your experiences and those of your team members, review your notes and look for trends or stories that jump off the page at you. Consider the following questions as you seek to create your maxim:

- Is there a story with strong emotional pull that best exemplifies how you will remind yourself to constantly challenge and inspire your team?
- Will that story serve as a stimulating mechanism to invest in your team's growth?
- Do any of these memories quickly capture your ideal of how a leader should develop his or her people?

The story, quote, or image you provide as the answer to these questions is the basis for your maxim. If you are passionate about gardening and feel as good when you tend to your plants as you do when you tend to your people's growth, you might have a maxim like "Tend to the garden." That connection—helping your people grow with the same care and attention you give your garden—can be a powerful reminder to invest in their development. Such a maxim links the positive emotions associated with your gardening to the positive actions of caring for your team. Again, seek to strip your resonant story down to something simple and easy to understand. It has to fit on that one piece of paper with all your other maxims, so guard against its becoming lengthy. Capture your thoughts on paper, then take some time away from them. When you return to those notes, see what connections you can make between those ideas or which stories resonate most for you. Write that thought or reminder down as your draft maxim. Once you have that draft, evaluate how strong it is as a maxim. Ask yourself these questions:

- Will this maxim encourage me to take calculated risks for the sake of my team's growth and development?
- When I read this maxim, am I quickly reminded how important it is to create a positively challenging environment for my people?
- Will adherence to this maxim prevent me from giving people only work of which I know they are 100 percent capable?
- When my team members hear me explain this maxim, will they understand how committed I am to helping them develop?

Your answers to these questions should all be "yes." When you are able to answer "yes" to all these questions, you are done writing your maxim for developing your people. Write that quote, image, or statement down in Appendix B.

To recap: people expect to grow and be challenged at work. Your responsibility as their leader is to create that environment for them. You must calculate the risks of putting people in stretch roles and take those chances when appropriate. You have the power to give or deny them growth opportunities at work, and if you do not create those opportunities for them, either they will get frustrated and have low morale or they will seek challenging growth opportunities outside your organization. If your development maxim reminds you to take those risks, you improve your chances of retaining and motivating talented people.

You must also provide coaching and feedback to the members of your team. Regardless of whether someone is in a stretch role or not, you need to provide guidance on a regular basis. It is easy to avoid difficult conversations, but doing so only makes subsequent conversations that much harder. Both you and your team members will benefit from your defining a maxim that pushes you to correct poor performance sooner rather than later.

You have now completed articulating your philosophy for how you will lead your people. People want to work for a leader who cares about them and is invested in helping them grow—and if you have been rigorous in writing your maxims in this part of the book, you now can clearly articulate and demonstrate your commitment to that growth. Your maxims for leading your people will express the essence of your leadership style. They will provide reminders that your people are individuals and help you stay connected to their reality. Finally, they will prod you to regularly commit to and invest in your team's growth and development.

No one wants to be a faceless cog in a big machine. Your maxims will be a powerful reminder to challenge and inspire the talented and complex individuals who make up your team.

PART 5

[LEADING A BALANCED LIFE]

CHAPTER 19

[DEFINING BALANCE]

We live in a stressful world. Business moves at an unprecedented pace and seems to speed up every day. Globalization and technology have introduced new challenges and opportunities into our lives. Retirement looms ahead of us. Commitments to family and friends suffer at the hands of our to-do list. We are in a constant state of high alert, ready to react to the next crisis looming right around the corner. All these dynamics conspire to stress us out.

Stress and fatigue break you down. They add to your waistline, clog your arteries, sap your energy, ruin your complexion, and generally run you into the ground. They can also derail your life and career. If you are burned out, you are worthless. You are worthless to your team, your family, your friends, and yourself. No one wants to work with or be around a tired, frazzled husk of a person whose once vibrant self has succumbed to the pressures of the world.

In an effort to reduce the stress we feel, we wave our arms and declare we want a balanced life. The problem is, we never define what that balance means. Also, we fail to achieve balance because we are driven. We enjoy our work. We believe the world will fall apart if we are not there to hold it together. The biggest reason we do not achieve balance is because we do not focus on it. Although balance is not on our work progress reviews, we must remember how important it is to our lives, both at work and outside of work.

WHAT IT MEANS TO BE BALANCED

The first step toward living a balanced life is realizing that both your life *and* your work need to be in balance. Many times we perceive this balanced life concept as pertaining only to not working late or on weekends. That is but one aspect of balance. Another aspect is doing work you enjoy. If work sucks, life sucks. You probably spend more time at your workplace than you do with your family and friends. To achieve balance in your work, you need to define the most rewarding aspects of your job. This definition ties back to feeling challenged and effective in the work you do. Work balance consists of working on enough of the things you love to do to balance out the things you dislike doing but have to put up with at your workplace. For example, if you love innovation and hate filling out expense reports, you must ensure that you have enough hours of your day dedicated to innovative activities to balance out the monotony of filling out expense reports. If the mix of your work shifts too far toward expense reporting, you will be out of balance at work. Of course this is an oversimplified example, but I am sure you get the point.

Creating maxims for balance at work requires you to define what is or is not acceptable behavior for you, your boss, your coworkers, and your team. If you focus on finding work you enjoy and have passion for, achieving work balance will naturally follow. There is powerful guidance on this point in the saying (often attributed to Confucius), "Choose a job you love, and you will never have to work a day in your life." Your maxims should help you consistently steer yourself toward work you love and away from work you do not. You will know you have achieved work balance when you feel excited, engaged, and motivated the vast majority of the time you are working. The days will seem to fly by, and you will feel like you are consistently in a strong positive rhythm. This mental state results from having a healthy portion of enjoyable tasks on your plate.

You will know you are out of balance when large parts of your day are filled with frustrating tasks. You will lack energy and enthusiasm, and time will seem to move at a crawl. You will find yourself railing against going to work on a daily basis. Yes, other factors can contribute to these feelings—major layoffs, micromanaging bosses, or other office turmoil. But, in general, when you find yourself feeling this awful feeling for more than a month straight, you do not have balance.

A wise man once told me the following, and I have tried to live by it:

"If you dread going to the office for a week, you are having a bad week. If you dread it for a month, you need to reconsider what you are doing. If you dread it for two months, you need to get your resume out on the street. If you dread it for longer than two months and have done nothing about it, you have dug your own grave."

Fortunately, I have never had to get out the grave-digging shovel. I have changed jobs on several occasions for a multitude of reasons. I made some of those changes because I no longer felt challenged. Other times, work was consuming too much of my time and energy and I had nothing left to give once I left the office. Leaving each of those jobs was a difficult choice to make. I am glad I did it, because now I no longer work (in the sense of that Confucius-attributed saying). I love the work I do. It is a true joy to teach, write, and build businesses. Sure, there are menial tasks I have to perform in my role, but my work balance tips well in the direction of engagement and away from mindless, trivial tasks.

Of course, a big part of leading a balanced life is enjoying your time off from work and ensuring that you have time off in the first place. Yes, taking time away from work can be difficult. But the alternative is living your life as the burnt-out husk of a person we talked about earlier. Spending too much time at work is a dysfunctional behavior, and you need to find a way to correct it. Your maxims will serve as the mechanism for successfully achieving balance in your life.

PUTTING THINGS IN PERSPECTIVE

To lead a balanced life, you need to put things in perspective. When you get stressed out, your focus narrows and you can lose sight of the bigger picture. This can happen in a split second when an incident occurs. It can also manifest itself at a broader level when you get overly focused on your current situation and forget to evaluate your life longer-term. This narrow focus on what is in front of you can cause you to miss other opportunities or problems. It can also result in an inability to accurately assess the relative importance of whatever it is you are focusing on. Doing so can cause you to blow things out of proportion or make bad decisions that resolve your immediate concern at the expense of more important things.

For example, if I received a bad progress review because I made mistakes in some financial models I built, that bad review would likely become my focal point. I might see those poor marks on modeling as a threat to my career and my advancement. It is natural to focus on threats. Evolution has taught us this behavior. So I would naturally focus on that threat and how to neutralize it. I would stress out over my performance and try to figure out the root cause of my failures. I would devote substantial effort to getting better at financial modeling to avoid another bad progress review. I might enroll in online modeling courses, spend hours at my computer building practice models, and seek coaching in how to get better at what seems like a critical skill. Unfortunately, this excessive focus on an issue that caused me great distress may lead me to ignore the possibility that building financial models might not be the best kind of work for me. I might miss another part of my progress review—the one that praises me for my writing and communication skills. I might not hear the encouraging words about taking on a more challenging position in which I can apply these communication skills. All this happened because my focus narrowed on what I perceived to be the critical task at hand—fixing my modeling performance issue.

At its core, balance is a measure of where you devote your time and energy. Ideally your balance favors dedicating those two precious resources to things you love doing. When you lose perspective, you shift a disproportionate amount of time and energy to something that might not deserve it (like worrying about spreadsheet modeling skills). In doing so, you will have shifted that time and energy away from things that are more important to you in the grander scheme of things, but your focus on the immediate stressor prevents you from appreciating the negative effects of this energy shift. To get back in balance and reallocate your energies to more fulfilling pursuits, you need to put things back in perspective. If you have a way to quickly regain perspective, you will find it much easier and less stressful to achieve the balance you seek. To regain perspective, you must strengthen your ability to step outside of your situation and view it through a different lens. Your maxims on perspective will help you build these abilities.

WHERE TO START

You can effectively change your behavior and achieve balance by creating maxims that are realistic and actionable. These rules of behavior should be practical, easy to understand, and simple to enforce. They must also be strong enough to reach you at an emotional level. When you write your balanced life maxims, do not shy away from powerful or painful memories. It is unlikely that "No work on weekends" would be a strong enough maxim to get you to change your behavior. It is a good platitude, but it has no teeth. You can easily look at it and ignore it or rationalize it away with the notion you are too busy and it is only a little work on the weekend. It is another thing entirely when your maxim is "Dad, you missed my baseball game and I hit a home run!" With the latter you are much more inclined to feel and remember the emotional consequences of the work/life choices you make. The pain of missing an important part of your child's life will much more effectively change your behavior than an unemotional platitude will. As with all your maxims, it's essential to base them on emotionally powerful experiences.

There are three questions you need to answer to create your maxims for leading a balanced life:

- How will you define your boundaries?
- How will you keep things in perspective?
- What are you passionate about?

The maxims you build around these questions will enable you to balance your work so that you are working on enough things that excite and interest you. They will also help you put boundaries around how much working and how much living you do, help you regain perspective when you lose it, and keep you focused on the most important things in your life.

This last aspect of leadership is critical. Your leadership philosophy must encompass your entire life, not just your work life. This holistic approach is designed to create integrity and consistency in your leadership approach in any situation. It creates checks and balances between looking internally and externally; short term and long term; at work and at home. If you can have a consistent leadership approach in all these areas, you will be a more comfortable and effective leader. Leading a balanced life is a huge component of creating that natural and comfortable style. Let's get started.

CHAPTER 20

HOW WILL YOU DEFINE YOUR BOUNDARIES?

You are the only one who can protect your time and your interests. You have to establish "the line" you are not willing to cross or allow others to cross. Whether it is the number of hours you work, the work you do (and the work others do), or the physical layout of your workspace, there are parameters that are or are not comfortable for you. The problem is, no one knows where your line is until you tell them they have crossed it. Unless you let others know what your comfort zone is, they will superimpose their own on you. Nine times out of ten you will be dissatisfied with their choice. You have to set boundaries to establish those lines.

ESTABLISHING BOUNDARIES

As you think about defining your lines, take a moment to reflect on times you have felt taken advantage of at work. Think about what boundary was crossed that made you uncomfortable. Were you asked to work late? To miss a family event? To do work well below your skill level? Once you have a sense for where those boundaries are, you can begin defining your lines. You need a set of lines you are happy working inside of that defines the mix of work you do or do not do and set limits on how long you will work, when you will work, and how you will work. They are designed to help you achieve a mix of work you will be excited about doing.

I enjoy being challenged by my work. I also prefer to manage my own tasks, deadlines, and priorities. Obviously, I communicate those priorities and agree on them with my leaders, but in general I prefer to have more control over them rather than less. My maxim for defining the lines of my work style is

I'm going home. You're doing my job.

Here is the story behind that maxim.

In one role I had, I kept my to-do list on a big whiteboard across from my desk so I could have all the work I needed to do staring me in the face. It was a good way for me to see everything I had to do at a glance. One day my boss walked into my office and stood facing me with his back to my whiteboard. He started rattling off all the things I should be thinking about, all the projects I should be doing, and all the analyses I should be conducting. Every item he mentioned was already written somewhere on my whiteboard. Several times I tried to interrupt him to explain that I was on top of things, but I was unable to get a word in edgewise. I was getting extremely frustrated with being micro-managed. I decided it was time to make a statement. I calmly picked up my briefcase, put it on my desk, put my laptop in it, closed it, and shut off the light on my desk.

"What are you doing?"

"I'm going home. You're doing my job, so you don't need me."

He was confused by my statement. I asked him to turn around and look at my whiteboard. I pointed out that all the things he was asking for were already under way and under control. I explained to him that I like to manage my tasks and my team's priorities. I helped him understand that I found meaning and excitement in running my organization, and he came to realize that a large portion of my job satisfaction was tied to having the space to do my job.

Was my approach to clarifying this point high-risk? Yes. Was it potentially a career-limiting move? Definitely. Was it also a pointed way to define boundaries, responsibilities, and preferred management styles? Absolutely. Fortunately, I had a great relationship with my boss and he got the point. He apologized for micromanaging, and I apologized for being disrespectful. After that incident he gave me a great deal of room to operate, and the balance of my work was to my liking.

I take some measure of satisfaction from being competent at my job. I do not enjoy being micromanaged. One way I prevent that from happening is to clearly articulate and agree on responsibilities and boundaries with my managers. Sharing my maxim and explaining its origin is a simple yet effective way to broach that conversation.

Achieving personal balance is just as important as achieving work balance, and it is especially hard for people who love their work. If you love what you are working on, it is hard to step away from it. You may find all your time is being consumed by work, even though it does not feel like work. Creating simple yet strong boundaries and habits can help you balance the amount of time you spend at work and the amount you spend away from it. It is not just time, either. You must achieve a state in which your energy is balanced between work and life. If you restrict your hours at the office by working at a furious pace that saps all your energy, you will have no energy left to live your life away from the office. That approach defeats the purpose of trying to achieve balance. Think of it this way: do I perform as well when I do things away from the office as I do when I am at work—or even better? That perspective is what balance is all about.

I know a fellow entrepreneur who struggled with the "life" part of work-life balance. He dedicated every last ounce of energy he had to building a cool new business. Everything he worked on was exciting and interesting to him. When we had lunch, he could not stop talking about all the fantastic things going on in his business, but when I asked how things were at home, his tone became much more reserved. He explained how tired he was when he got home at night and how his son regularly said he missed him. The entrepreneur had not been sleeping well, and he had put on about fifteen pounds since I last saw him because his physical fitness regimen had lapsed. As he finished detailing his less-than-satisfying description of his home life, he said he wanted to achieve a better balance between work and home but he was at a loss for how he could do that.

I asked if he had experienced similar challenges when he was a "corporate guy," and he said no. He had had no problem making time for his family in the evenings. He would get in a solid workout every morning before heading to the office. He slept better and was generally happier, despite not particularly enjoying his corporate job.

As we talked about his corporate role, I asked him what had changed since he went out on his own. He said he was much happier with the work he was doing, but the variability in his schedule made it unpredictable and he found it difficult to establish a routine. He also felt a great deal of pressure to work on everything in front of him because he was solely responsible for the success of his business. He believed that if he did not drive hard and tackle every project, his business might fail.

"What would happen if you left work at 6:00 P.M. and did not work on any of the projects you normally would in the evening?" I asked.

"I guess I would end up working on those projects the next day. But the problem is, the next day is always packed with other stuff to do."

"Why don't you try shutting the computer at 7:00 P.M. every night for the next few weeks, then let's grab coffee and find out how things are going. You have to promise to hold yourself to that standard. Also, start your workouts again, and don't open your computer until after you have finished working out."

Initially he looked at me like I was crazy. But he reluctantly agreed to try the new approach. After several weeks we reconnected for coffee and I asked how things were going.

"I'm getting to spend time with my family now, at least. I feel better too because I'm working out again. I even lost a few pounds in the past few weeks. At first I panicked at the thought of not getting all that former 'evening' work done, but it's been weird. All those things I used to do at night don't seem to get done the next day. The odd part is, it isn't a big deal if they don't get done. They seem to remain on my to-do list, but there really are no consequences to not completing those things."

We discussed how the approach of walking away from the work at 7:00 P.M. was forcing him to prioritize. In the past he'd had no time constraints, so he did not have to make a choice about what work got done. His choice was instead one of what time he would finish. His limiting factor was the work, not the time. By being rigorous about sticking to a fixed schedule, he naturally began working on the most important things first to ensure that he completed them by his self-imposed 7:00 P.M. deadline. Lower-priority work automatically fell to the bottom of the list. His time with his family and his new workout regimen reduced his stress and helped him sleep better. The extra sleep made him more productive during the day, and a virtuous circle ensued.

At this point I offered him a challenge: "I'm thrilled to hear about your progress. Now how will you *ensure* that you stick to the new schedule and stop working when you are supposed to?" We discussed the maxims approach, and I asked if there was an image he had a pleasant association with related to leaving work.

He immediately said "Fred Flintstone!"

I confessed I did not know why he chose that particular cartoon character nor did I know how he was relating Fred Flintstone to leaving his office.

"When I was a kid, *The Flintstones* was my favorite cartoon. In the opening credits, the whistle blows and Fred sprints out of work to go home. He was excited to leave the office every day. I guess every time I think of *The Flintstones* I can't help but smile, and for some reason the image of Fred hurrying out of work at the closing whistle is the first thing that came to mind when you asked me that."

His maxim became

Fred Flintstone

It was a reminder to him to leave the office on time and to be happy he was going home. He had positive emotions related to that image, and it resonated for him every time he thought about it. After all these years, Fred Flintstone is still helping people enjoy their lives.

WRITING YOUR MAXIMS

You need to define your own lines regarding the work you do or do not do, time spent at work versus time spent away from it, and any other boundaries that make your work and life experience a pleasant one. These lines will form your maxims. You should be able to rely on them during stressful times to remind you of the behaviors that enable you to achieve balance.

First, define your work balance. Ask yourself the following questions and document your answers:

- What kind of work is required for you to be happy with your job? Which specific tasks or activities do you find the most fulfilling?
- What kind of work or which tasks would you love to eliminate from your daily routine?
- Which characteristics of your job would you like to maintain at all costs (such as flexibility, predictability, ambiguity, simplicity, complexity, independence)? In what kind of environment are you most productive?
- What characteristics of your job would you like to eliminate (for example, unpredictability, complexity, conflicting demands)? In which kinds of environments are you unproductive or unhappy?
- How do you prefer your coworkers, bosses, and team members to interact with you? How do you prefer they not interact? What pet peeves do you have regarding how others treat you?
- Is there anyone you know who has an outstanding balance of doing work they are thrilled with and work they do not enjoy? How do they achieve that mix of

work? What can you change about your own approach to work to better emulate them?

- Has there ever been a point in life in which you had a good work-life balance? What were the circumstances surrounding that situation that made it work?

Next, you need to explore how you will achieve life balance. Consider the following:

- Which aspects of your life feel out of balance? Health? Time with family? Your financial situation?
- In which aspects do you have a great balance?
- Do you have any mechanisms that keep things in balance? If so, what are they? For which areas do you need better mechanisms for maintaining your balance?
- Have there been instances in which you chose work over life and regretted that decision? Have there been times when you chose life over work and derived a great deal of satisfaction and happiness from that choice?
- Do you know anyone whose balance of work and life is fantastic? How could you create a similar balance for yourself? What would you have to change about your behaviors to make that happen?
- Do you know anyone who is all work and no life? How can you avoid becoming like that person?

Have any stories emerged as you've answered these questions? What about patterns? Do any of your examples hold special meaning for you? Choose one story or saying related to work balance and another tied to life balance. For example, if you missed your son's first birthday party because you felt you had to catch up on work on a Saturday, your maxim focused on achieving life balance might be "William's first birthday." Pick one aspect of each story that immediately reminds you of everything about it. Distill each of the two aspects to a pithy phrase or sentence that will quickly bring the story to the forefront of your mind. Each phrase should have the ability to get you to change your behavior in a way consistent with how you want to "show up" at work and at home.

These statements are your maxims for defining the boundaries in which you live and work. They are a summation of the things you consider important in your life. If those things are important, you should be able to give a resounding "yes!" to the following questions:

- If I do not have an acceptable mix of work I enjoy doing and work I do not enjoy, will this maxim encourage me to try to change that balance?
- If I explain this maxim to my boss and coworkers, will they quickly understand my boundaries at the office?
- Will this maxim pry me away from my desk even when I feel overloaded at work?
- Does the story behind this life balance maxim set my lifestyle boundaries in a clear and compelling manner?
- Will my boss and team accept and support the decisions I make related to a balanced life once they understand this story?

When you can answer "yes" to these questions, your maxims are strong enough to change your behavior. Once you have two maxims that work for you, record them in Appendix B.

Your balance maxims must withstand the pressures that work puts on you. Invariably you will be asked to take on tasks at work that are less than exciting. Your work balance maxim is a vehicle for pushing back and trying to get an acceptable mix of exciting and unexciting work. Your life balance maxim must have the power to make you close the laptop and go home. The emotional reaction it causes is the source of its power over your workday. That emotional link is the key to determining whether you will walk away from the computer or not.

Balancing your time and energy requires a great deal of effort. If that energy shifts to tasks you do not enjoy, you will find yourself unhappy and eventually stressed out. Creating and maintaining good boundaries helps prevent the pressures of work from pushing you out of balance. Your maxims are simply the articulation of those boundaries and serve as a way to communicate them to others and reinforce them on a regular basis.

CHAPTER 21

[HOW WILL YOU KEEP THINGS IN PERSPECTIVE?]

Many of us take the events in our lives way too seriously. Anything and everything ends up being viewed as serious and important. Little things become larger than they really are and can seem more critical than truly important things. When you take things too seriously, you lose perspective. Losing perspective creates stress. Stress takes a real toll on your health and ultimately can shorten your life.

When the human body is stressed, all attention is pulled in and focused on the stressor. Vision becomes tunneled, and "extraneous" information is blocked to enable focus on the perceived threat. It is biology at work. Going back to the days before recorded history, when a caveman saw a saber-toothed cat emerge from the woods, he ignored anything not related to getting away from that threat. Those same instincts have remained with us for thousands of years. When we perceive a threat we focus on it to the exclusion of everything else around us. That reaction is a defense mechanism that prevents distractions from taking our attention away from the survival task at hand. The problem is, this physiological reaction causes us to lose perspective. This focusing instinct does not serve us as well as it did the caveman because there are not too many saber-toothed cats prowling the cubicles of the office.

If you examine how this instinctive reaction to a stressor manifests itself in the modern world, you will see how dysfunctional it can be. Imagine you are the brand manager responsible for your company's website. When you see a formatting error on your website (which, remember, you are responsible for), you realize millions of consumers might notice it and they will think less of your brand, which means your sales will drop, which will crater your stock price, which will destroy your 401(k). OH MY GOD YOU'LL NEVER BE ABLE TO RETIRE! See how quickly that happens?

STAYING FOCUSED ON WHAT'S IMPORTANT

When you are stressed, you will focus on the perceived threat in front of you, whether that threat is a predator or a formatting error on your company's website. Your adrenaline will surge and your thoughts will race. Typically those thoughts will run toward the worst possible scenario imaginable. To avoid the stress associated with allowing little things to seem big, you need to take a step back and regain your perspective. Maxims are a helpful tool for doing just that. They serve as touchstones to reground you during stressful moments when you are losing your composure over trivial events and bring you back to reality.

There have been times in my career when I was in a high-stress role. Being a type-A personality in those situations made me susceptible to losing perspective quite easily. Fortunately, I have used several maxims at different points in my career to keep me grounded and to bring me back to center when I am knocked off balance. I have also used those maxims to bring members of my team and coworkers back to a centered state when they get carried away by an issue and lose focus.

The first of these maxims is

Burger King is hiring.

I had a great boss at one point who always kept himself centered and grounded. He was the quintessential unflappable guy. One particular day I went into his office to bemoan some typical corporate problem that was causing me a significant amount of stress. My boss let me complain for a while, and once I had expended all my energy, he looked me dead in the eye and said, "Burger King is hiring."

I blinked a few times as I tried to process his comment. When I was unable to extract meaning from the statement, he offered an explanation.

"From the sound of it, you're frustrated with the way things are going. I don't blame you. I would be frustrated too. If you hate it here, you should find another job. If you're interested in finding that next job, I thought you should know Burger King is hiring. I'm sure you would have a lot less frustration to deal with if your role consisted of flipping burgers all day long. Now that you know they're hiring, does this problem seem like one worth quitting your job over?"

With my newfound perspective, the issue I was complaining about no longer seemed as important as I was making it out to be. It certainly was not bad enough to quit my job over. Once I had regained my perspective, I was able to approach solving the problem more rationally and logically. Since this incident I have used "Burger King is hiring" many times both to recenter myself and to help members of my team regain perspective.

The second maxim I use to keep or regain perspective is not even a quote or a statement. It is an object. My maxim is

A Burger King crown

This maxim came into being during a miserable week. By the time Friday morning rolled around, things were crazy and I was ready to snap like a dry twig. To escape the morning's insanity, I broke my habit of eating at my desk; I went out for lunch. I ended up at Burger King. They had a pile of cardboard crowns on the counter. I grabbed one and adjusted it to my head. I wore the crown. People looked at me. I looked back. They went about their business.

I returned to the office still wearing the crown. I proclaimed myself King Mike. My coworkers gave me quizzical looks. I looked back like there was nothing going on. My wearing of the crown at work unnerved some of them. Others laughed with me. Their day was a little brighter because they saw the humor in it. I attended a steering committee meeting that afternoon. I was still wearing the crown. I was engaged in the conversation and contributed several thoughts on the projects we were reviewing. Some attendees suffered massive cognitive dissonance to see me wearing the crown while discussing the r-squared of an analysis. The combination of the crown and intelligent inquiry was too much of an inconsistency for them to process.

After the meeting, a colleague asked, "Why are you wearing the crown? Did you lose a bet? Why do you have that thing on?"

I replied with a slight smirk, "Because."

"Because why?"

"Because. If you don't get it and have to ask that question again, you will never get it, which is really sad."

He shook his head and walked away. He never got it.

Others did get it and laughed. They realized if I could take myself a little less seriously and shrug off the stress of a crazy work week, they could too. They saw I was still engaged in my work, but having perspective was important too. I wore the crown the rest of the day. I have, on occasion, gotten it out once or twice over the past few years, and it has always made my day better. Every time I see a Burger King crown, I am reminded of a great memory, and I find myself with a little smile on my face. The maxim has strong emotional meaning for me and actually physiologically decreases my anxiety.

The third maxim I have used at times to keep things in perspective is

It's only [blank].

inserting whatever is stressing me out at that particular moment into that blank. My colleague Lynn taught me this maxim. Kevin, a member of Lynn's team, had implemented a new analytical model in the call center. As he watched the call center metrics post-implementation, things were not going well. The longer he watched, the worse things got. The worse things got, the more nervous and anxious Kevin became. Eventually he decided he needed to roll back his model and revert to the prior version he had been using pre-implementation. He scrambled down the hall to Lynn's office and excitedly told her things were not going well. Kevin pleaded for immediate IT support to make the change. He was talking a mile a minute. As he frantically rattled off all the steps he needed to take to make the changes, Lynn held up her hand in front of his face and said, "It's only credit cards."

Her statement derailed Kevin's speeding train of thought. She continued: "Look, I know things are messed up, but there's no reason to lose your mind like this. Remember—it's only credit cards. That's what we do. Credit cards. Not brain surgery; not returning astronauts from the moon; not solving world hunger. We do credit cards. If we don't get it fixed this instant, no one is going to die. Don't worry. We'll fix it. Catch your breath, calm down, and go take care of things. When you freak out, you freak out the team. When everyone freaks out, mistakes happen. Given that we have already made some mistakes, there is no sense in compounding the problem because you cannot regain your composure. Now say it with me: 'It's only credit cards.'"

I don't know whether it was Lynn's lecture or the "it's only" statement that got Kevin to calm down, but her efforts were successful. Once Kevin regained his composure, he went about his business and took care of the problem at hand.

Since witnessing this interaction between Lynn and Kevin, I have used "It's only [blank]" in many situations, both to regain my composure as well as to help members of my team do the same. I have said "It's only fertilizer," "It's only taxes," and "It's only sixty-five thousand words," to name but a few. Every single time, that statement has helped me take a step back from the problem I was hyperfocused on and tackle that problem with a clearer head and calmer demeanor.

Dan, a Chinese-American director at a financial services firm, had a simple maxim that helped him and those around him maintain perspective:

Calm

Dan explained it both humorously and eloquently. "It's pretty hard to miss that I'm Asian, and even though I've lived in the U.S. my entire life, people always ask silly stereotypical questions like if I practice tai chi or martial arts. I always laugh at their expressions when I tell them I grew up in the mean streets of Philadelphia. That said, I have found that I'm able to exude calm during chaotic situations, and people around me respond to my calming influence. My ability to get everyone around me to stop, take a breath, and relax reduces stress and helps me and the team put things in perspective. So that's my maxim—calm. It's only one word, but it reminds me to stop, breathe, focus, and then act."

As Dan shared his story, it was clear how his demeanor and this maxim combined to create a powerful means of regaining perspective.

WRITING YOUR MAXIMS

You have seen how I regain and retain my perspective. How do you keep yours? Staying in balance requires you to stay centered in your thoughts and your behaviors. When stressors come along and knock you off balance, the faster you can regain your center, the more effectively you can deal with the issue at hand. Your ability to quickly compose yourself is one of the most powerful antistress defenses at your disposal.

Spend a few moments writing down your answers to the following questions. They will help you identify reminders or triggers designed to get you back in balance. These questions should help you identify stories or events to which you can compare a stressful event in order to put your current stressor in perspective. These questions may also enable you to create a lens through which you can look at stressful situations, helping you realize that you may be making a bigger deal of the stressor than you should.

- When life gets stressful, how do you regain your composure?
- Has there ever been a time when you were upset and someone else calmed you down? What did they say or do that helped you relax?
- What is the worst thing that has ever happened to you? How could you compare that terrible thing to another stressful situation you have faced?
- During a crisis, how do you remember to set a calm example for your team and others around you?
- What practices do you use to regain your center (such as breathing, exercising, meditating)?
- Is there someone you know who is uncommonly calm during chaotic times? Are there things that person says or does to create calm?
- Do you know someone who freaks out in the face of stress? Are there behaviors that person demonstrates that you would never want to exhibit?

As you reflect on your answers to these questions, look for cues you can use to remind yourself to keep things in perspective. For example, if the worst thing that has ever happened to you is the loss of a job, a possible maxim for you is "It's not as bad as losing my job." If you know someone who is the calm in the eye of any storm, perhaps something that person has said that effectively calms others down can be your maxim. In writing this maxim, you are looking for something that forces you to take a step back from the stressful situation at hand so you can assess it and respond to it with a cool head and a calm heart.

Once you have come up with a first draft of this maxim, evaluate how powerful it is by asking yourself these questions:

- If I am in a stressful situation, will thinking about this maxim help me stay calm?
- If something happens that seems terrible, will this maxim help me look at the event more objectively and less excitedly?
- Will this maxim prevent me from taking events (and myself) too seriously? Can it help me lighten up and enjoy the things going on around me?
- Will this maxim help me differentiate between the seemingly important and the actually important?

If you can answer all these questions with an unequivocal "yes," then you have written a solid maxim for keeping things in perspective and you should record it in Appendix B. If not, keep refining the maxim until you are satisfied with it.

In a stressful situation it is easy to lose perspective and focus on the immediate crisis in front of you. In doing so, you lose your balance, and all sorts of unhappiness and poor performance can follow. Even worse, your team senses your stress and begins demonstrating its own signs of stress. By creating a maxim (or two) that helps you step back from the stressor and regain both perspective and balance, you now can deal with the stressful situation more effectively while simultaneously being a calming influence for your team. When you restore calm and perspective, you will find you are generally happier and less stressed. The maxims you've created now, during relative calm, will help you restore calm during the inevitable chaos ahead of you.

CHAPTER 22

[WHAT ARE YOU PASSIONATE ABOUT?]

It is easy to get wrapped up in your work. If you have chosen your profession well, you are darn good at what you do and take a great deal of satisfaction in doing it well. Unfortunately, it is easy to forget that there are other people out there who want some of your time. Your family and friends need your attention. There are also other passions worth pursuing outside the workplace. Taking part in activities you enjoy will keep you centered and add meaning and fulfillment to your life.

Unless you have a mechanism to tear yourself away from your workplace, you may find yourself trapped in the mindset of "I'll do [insert enjoyable thing here] this weekend when I'm off work" or "I'll do that when I retire" or "I'll get to that someday." Someone who reads my blog shared a great maxim on this point: "Someday is not a day of the week." We would all do well to keep this in mind and act accordingly. My great-grandfather adopted a quote as his maxim to remind him to live life. He always said, "Enjoy life now because you'll be a long time dead." He did not coin the phrase, but he used it frequently. The saying has made its way through a few generations of my family as something we say on a semiregular basis. Regardless of how it is phrased, the key point is that we must have balance in our lives, which entails living our lives while there is still breath in our lungs.

MAKING TIME FOR YOUR LIFE

Without a frequent reminder to do what you truly enjoy and have passion for, you might not notice your life slipping by. This reminder will help you balance your choices between work and life. Failing to have that reminder and abide by it has profound consequences. You run the risk of waking up one day only to find you have missed hundreds, if not thousands, of opportunities to be happy. The sooner you write a maxim to remind you to keep balance in your life and pursue your passions, the less likely it is that you will miss those opportunities and the more likely it is that you will enjoy your life.

My maxim for reminding me to enjoy my time away from the office is

A bad day of fishing is better than a good day of work.

Sure, I read it on a bumper sticker somewhere a long time ago. It is not original, but it does have a significant emotional effect on me, as all good maxims should. See, I love to fish. It is not about whether or not I catch something. The act of being on the water and taking in the natural world around me is what I enjoy. Fishing helps me decompress from the stresses at work and reminds me to appreciate my time away from the office.

I have not only applied this maxim at the end of the work day—I have applied it *during* the work day. On one occasion, it had been a particularly harrowing week. It was filled with progress reviews, steering committees, meetings, and ridiculous "reply all" emails. By Friday afternoon I was close to my wit's end. It was a beautiful April day. My work was "done" by all rights. It was time to catch my breath. I went out for lunch, and when I returned to the office, I realized I had my fishing pole in my car. As I looked at my tackle, I remembered *A bad day of fishing is better than a good day at work.* I grabbed my fishing pole and my tackle box and walked to the lake on our office campus. The lake was surrounded by several buildings containing my colleagues. I started fishing. I began catching fish—nice ones. I lost myself in the afternoon sun and breeze. I was out there a solid two hours. I finally took a break from fishing and looked at our offices. Many of my colleagues were lining the windows watching me with incredulous looks on their faces.

I packed up my stuff and went inside. One individual who saw me fishing said, "Are you crazy? You're going to get fired."

"Why?" I asked.

"You were fishing! It's Friday afternoon!"

"Yeah. So? My work is done. I'm ahead of schedule on most things. I needed a little time to decompress."

"You're crazy."

"Am I? Let me ask you this: I was outside recharging my batteries, basking in the beautiful weather, and enjoying a great afternoon of fishing. You were in here answering email and working on spreadsheets. Who's the crazy one?"

He didn't say another word.

Then it happened. A few people packed up early. They said they were going to head out and spend time with their kids, with friends, or at the gym. The perspective on what was important spread quickly. In this instance my maxim changed not only my behavior but the behavior of those around me. I like to think I helped put the world back in balance that day, even if only a tiny bit.

The more I have tried to live up to this maxim over time, the happier I have been with the results. As in the incident I just related, it has benefited those around me too. I love fishing not only for the calm of the nature surrounding me but also because I spend a significant amount of time with my son when I fish. He and I have created a substantial number of great memories on the fishing excursions we have taken together. We have caught everything from bluegill in local ponds to trout in Colorado to wahoo in Hawaii to monster bass in Florida. I can clearly remember every smile on his face when he hooked into and landed a great fish. I treasure every minute of every one of those trips. My relationship with him is much stronger because of the time we have spent on the water together. Ever since he was four I have found times for us to slip away and fish. I have tried to teach him life lessons and maxims during those times together. When he gets older and, I hope, creates his own set of maxims, I also hope that one thing I have always said to him makes the list. Every time we are in the car on the way to fish, we share the following exchange:

I ask, "Why do we go fishing?"

He replies, "To go fishing."

I then ask, "And if we catch fish?"

He replies, "It's a bonus!"

I have reinforced this concept for him over many years because I want him to do a better job than I have at creating and enjoying down time. I am hopeful he carries this mindset forward into adulthood and achieves a better sense of balance in his life than I have in mine at times.

My love of fishing and the corresponding maxim reminds me to take vacations and time off to spend with my family. Over the years I have done a lousy job on this front. I look back and regret all the years I put work ahead of vacation and time away. There always seemed to be a good excuse for not taking the time off. Upon reflection, all those excuses were lame and ridiculous.

Since I have focused on achieving more balance, I have relied on my maxim more frequently. I have seen my behavior change for the better. While fishing is a component of and an excuse to go on vacation, the real passion it unlocks is spending time with people I love who love me in return. This maxim keeps my urge to work in check and helps me focus on what is truly important in life. That one straightfor-ward sentence encourages me to commit to time away from the office doing the things I enjoy with people I love. This maxim is a consistent reminder of why I work as hard as I do—so I can have the flexibility in my schedule and the cash in my bank account to do amazing things with the people closest to me. Reminding myself that a bad day of fishing is better than a good day of work gets me to reprioritize where

I spend my time. It pries me away from the office in pursuit of activities that have meaning at a higher level. And fortunately, on most of our fishing trips we not only enjoy our time on the water but we usually catch a ton of fish. Let me tell you—a great day of fishing kicks the crap out of a great day at work!

Victor, the vice president of a financial services firm, says his maxim is "Work buys adrenaline." He explained to me how although he has been very successful from both a career and a financial standpoint, all his efforts are focused on one outcome: adrenaline. Victor loves to skydive, rock climb, go whitewater rafting, ski, surf, and a variety of other exciting activities. Those activities are not cheap. He said he feels most alive when he is out performing these activities, and the rush of adrenaline he gets from doing them is the reason he works so hard. "Taking a trip to surf in Hawaii or ski in Colorado is pretty expensive, so I work really hard to make a great paycheck. But it's not about the paycheck. The pay is a means to an end, and that end is the rush I get from doing all these crazy outdoor activities and the memories associated with those amazing trips." His maxim keeps him focused on working hard *and* prevents him from forgetting the passion that drives him.

WRITING YOUR MAXIMS

A good maxim will remind you that work is a means to an end. It will enable you to make better decisions about where you allocate your time and energy to ensure that you have a balance between the work you do and the things you love in life.

You might think that creating your maxim for achieving balance in your life will be simple. I will caution you that it is quite difficult. The simplicity stems from your having a deep understanding of what you are excited about in life. You likely have favored hobbies or pastimes that come readily to mind. It is easy to zero in on those as the source of raw material for creating this maxim. The difficult part is writing your maxim in such a way that the emotional trigger to take action is powerful enough to overcome the inertia of your work life. If the maxim cannot get you to step away from the laptop and leave the workplace, it is worth less than the one piece of paper it is written on. You must find an emotional trigger that creates a visceral reaction inside of you.

As you write this maxim, I invite you to consider anything and everything that can serve as a reminder of why you work. Think about what you want to get out of life. Imagine a conversation with your grandchildren many years down the road, when they ask you what your fondest memories are. I will bet during that conversation you will not be discussing spreadsheets and steering committee presentations. Search within yourself and recall those out-of-work events that fill you with joy because you had that experience. Think about decisions you made to work instead of live and select the moments that fill you with regret because you chose work instead of life.

Now that you are in the right frame of mind to write this maxim, consider the following questions and document your answers on some paper.

- If all your time was yours to do with as you pleased, what would you do?
- If money was no object and you no longer had to work, how would you spend your time?
- Is there one fantastic choice you have made where you put your life first and your work second?
- Is there one terrible choice you have made where you chose to work instead of attending to something important in your personal life?
- When you are forced to choose between work and life, what is your deciding factor for making that choice?

Once you have answered these questions, you need to identify the event, image, quote, or other trigger that is the most powerful reminder of why you work. Select the one that has a strong enough emotional pull to make you step away from your office and pursue the things in life that hold the most meaning for you. As with all your other maxims, distill this concept down to its bare essentials. Make it a pointed reminder of what is important in your life. For example, if you are passionate about travel, and all the money you earn is a means of funding your trips, a montage of photos from the best trips you have taken or a photo of the one place you want to go more than any other can be your maxim. That passion for travel can be summarized by a set of images. Those pictures can serve to remind you of what you are excited about, and it can help you make choices consistent with following that passion. Remember, you need a maxim that will guide your choices so that when you face a choice between work and life you will be happy with your decision.

Once you are satisfied with the maxim, test it to see if it is powerful enough for you to live by. Evaluate it according to the following questions:

- When I am faced with a difficult choice between work and life, will this maxim help me quickly decide which one to choose?
- Does the maxim generate strong feelings within me such that it can motivate me to step away from my work to pursue other things that are important to me?
- If I explain the maxim to my team and coworkers, will they easily understand why I make the choices I make with respect to work and life? Will they respect those choices and the boundaries accompanying them?
- If I live my life according to this maxim, will I be happy with the choices I make and not have any regrets about those choices when all is said and done?

You should be able to answer all these questions in the affirmative. If you cannot, go back and sharpen your pencil. Retool that maxim until it is a compelling reminder of what is important to you in your life. Write it in a way that you cannot help but be moved by it every time you read it. Once you've finished, add it to your other completed maxims in Appendix B.

Congratulations! You've done it. You have completed the leadership maxims creation process. If you have been rigorous and thoughtful as you have gone through the preceding chapters, you have a powerful first version of your maxims articulated in the appendix of this book. This version will evolve as you live and use your maxims and reevaluate them over time.

I hope that after going through the maxims creation process you have an appreciation for how the four aspects of leadership—leading yourself, the thinking, your people, and a balanced life—work together to give you a complete picture of who you are and who you want to be as a leader. By considering all four aspects as major components of your leadership philosophy, you are ensuring that your approach to leadership is well-rounded and consistent in all areas of your life. That consistency eliminates confusion and strips away unproductive façades. By embedding your personal story in your leadership maxims, you have taken a huge step toward being more authentic, because you are letting your team know who you truly are as a person rather than hiding behind buzzwords and lingo. You are sharing the experiences that have defined who you are as a person and as a leader. The transparency and clarity you can now provide others by sharing your maxims should reduce confusion and mistrust and promote stronger relationships between you and the members of your team. Your maxims will also serve as touchstones to guide your behavior in a purposeful direction toward always being the leader you want to be.

PART 6

[MAKING IT REAL]

CHAPTER 23

[LIVING YOUR MAXIMS]

At the beginning of this process, when I told you there was a way to clearly define yourself as a leader on a single page, it may have seemed like a difficult task. Perhaps even impossible. But you've done it. And it was simple, wasn't it? Okay, perhaps "simple" is too strong a word. Let's use "straightforward" instead. Articulating your leadership philosophy does not have to be complicated.

The hard parts of the leadership maxims process are the introspection about and the personalization of your philosophy. It can be difficult to remove the veil of "professionalism" and accept your own humanity. It is scary to put the *real* you out there for everyone to see. It is much easier to hide behind terms like synergies, value maximization, and employee engagement. It is exponentially more powerful to expose the real you to the people you are supposed to lead. That is what it means to be authentic, and the more authentic and direct your leadership philosophy is, the more powerful it will be.

YOUR ONE PIECE OF PAPER

I hope you have been writing your first draft of your maxims in Appendix B as you have worked your way through this book. If you haven't because you wanted to read the entire method before applying it, I encourage you to go back to the beginning of the book to start documenting your maxims. This book is useful only if you use it to put your maxims on paper and create a physical reminder of what you stand for as a leader. If you don't, you are much less likely to use your philosophy to guide your daily behavior once you put this book down and forget about it. You need that one piece of paper staring you in the face every day to reinforce your maxims and keep you headed in the right direction.

Assuming you have written all your maxims down, take a look at them. What do you think? Your maxims should be fifteen to twenty-five bullet points, phrases, lyrics, images, or sentences. If you have long and complex draft maxims or if they do not speak to who you are as a unique individual, something is not right. Each and every one should evoke an emotion or remind you of a story. They need to be as personal as you can possibly make them. No corporate-speak or buzzwords allowed. Focus on genuine stories and direct, easy-to-understand language. If you cannot understand a maxim in one quick glance, it is too complex. If you cannot relate a personal story behind the maxim when you share it with someone else, it is not personal enough.

You may find that initially using your maxims feels awkward. They may not resonate much for you. If they do not strike you as powerful statements that represent who you are as a leader, it may be because you are trying to fool yourself into being something you are not. As you read the first version of your maxims, ask yourself whether they truly capture who you are and who you want to be as a person and as a leader. If they do not, you are not being honest with yourself. If that is the case, you will definitely not apply your maxims on a daily basis, so you need to reevaluate and revise them. If your maxims do resonate with you, you are well on your way to becoming the authentic leader you want to be.

LIVING YOUR LEADERSHIP MAXIMS

Having your maxims on one piece of paper is powerful. Eventually they will change your behavior and you can take massive strides toward being the leader and the person you want to be. Your maxims will be there for you during times of uncertainty. They will keep you on course. They will be a constant reminder of what is important to you and how you want to show up in the world.

Once you have written the first version of your maxims, you can start living by them. Remember, a maxim is nothing more than a principle or rule of conduct. These are *your* rules. You set them for yourself. You have to live with them, and you will be a better leader if you abide by them.

Your maxims will help you make better decisions and choices, especially during difficult times. They will keep you on track to reach your goals, and they will guide your behaviors along the way. Your maxims will serve as a tool for setting and maintaining standards for both yourself and your organization. Most important, your maxims will humanize you and help you build the trust critical to running a high-performing team.

I have found the maxims approach to be a powerful tool for leading my teams as well as managing my performance. My maxims are aspirational. I set exceedingly high standards for myself because I enjoy the challenge and I want to be a better person and leader than I currently am. I do not always live up to the standards I set for myself through my maxims. As you have seen through my examples, I have fallen short of those standards on many occasions. I am not proud of that fact. What I am proud of, however, is leading an examined life and constantly evaluating my performance and behavior against a standard I set for myself. I am able to admit my shortcomings and failures against a measuring post I have defined. Those admissions and the resolve to get better the next time are a great source of pride and strength for me. Without my maxims, I know that self-examination, evaluation, and introspection would be difficult. I am a better leader and a better person than I would be without them.

Find opportunities to refer to your maxims in conversations with members of your team. Once your people know and understand your maxims, these become a vehicle for reinforcing your values and standards not only for yourself but for the team as well. You also need to keep them fresh in your own mind. Print them out. Laminate them. Put them someplace you will see them every day. Pin a copy up on your wall. Carry a copy with you in a notebook or in your wallet. Make sure your maxims are a permanent fixture in your life. You might also consider reading your maxims once a day. Spend the two minutes it will take to read your one piece of paper while you sip your morning coffee or tea. It does not have to be a big, elaborate exercise. All you need to do is remind yourself what your standards are as you set about your work day. It is a much better use of those two minutes than reading the latest news about movie stars or watching the newest funny cat video on the Internet. I promise that if you invest the time in your maxims you will quickly begin receiving the dividends from that document. No matter how you decide to put your maxims into practice, make certain that one piece of paper is never far from your mind. That way, when you are presented with a challenging situation, your maxims will be within arm's reach. The proximity of that one piece of paper to your point of decision will enable you to rely on your maxims with little effort. And of course, over time you will have some or all of them committed to memory—and you'll be able to easily access the powerful emotions and memories associated with each maxim. You will be able to quickly apply your maxims in that situation, thereby guiding your behavior and decisions toward goals you previously set for yourself. It is the consistent practice of what you have preached that will lead you to the achievement of your goals.

As I have matured and changed over time, my maxims have done the same. That is called growth. In Appendix A you will find a copy of my maxims. Some of them are old and have either been replaced or improved upon. I have included them in the list for your benefit so you can see maxims that have worked for me in the past. As you grow as a leader and take on new challenges, those situations will call for new approaches, and your maxims too will change. Revisiting your maxims at turning points in your career can help you adjust your path accordingly. I encourage you to refer to them regularly and reevaluate your maxims once or twice a year to see if any need to be changed, removed, or added to your list. The changes in your maxims are reflective of your own growth and development, and this exercise will help you reexamine the kind of leader you say you want to be. It will be an opportunity to evaluate your performance relative to a standard you have set for yourself. Although sometimes it is necessary to drop a maxim because it is no longer relevant to your personal or professional situation, typically when you remove a maxim from your list it is because the behaviors it drives have become ingrained in who you are as a person and as a leader, so you no longer need a reminder to behave in that manner. When a maxim becomes a part of your leadership DNA and you no longer need that statement on a piece of paper, you have experienced true growth.

Use a regular review process to assess how you have grown and where you have not. For areas still requiring improvement, consider adding new maxims or refining your current ones to drive the behavioral change you desire. A good practice to build is to review your maxims every time your performance is reviewed. Most organizations have a twice-yearly performance appraisal process, and many people write self-appraisals as part of that process. If you go through this process in your organization, make a personal review of your maxims part of your self-appraisal. You do not have to share that review with others. Take a few hours and review every maxim in detail. Ask yourself these questions as part of that process:

- Is this maxim still relevant to my personal and professional situation?
- Do the emotions related to this maxim still guide my behavior in a positive way?
- Does this maxim still point me in my desired direction?
- Is there a better image, story, or quote that will more powerfully guide my behavior than this maxim currently does?
- Have I internalized the behaviors and beliefs underlying this maxim to a point where I no longer require the maxim to guide me in this arena?
- Are there new directions I want to go in or new goals I want to achieve that I do not yet have a maxim for?
- Are there new behaviors, stories, or maxims I need to add to this list?

Your maxims will become more natural the more you use them. It is consistent and frequent use that will drive behavior change over time. During the regular review process you should see yourself growing in measurable ways. As maxims come off your list or change or as others are added, you will be able to see where you have internalized desired behaviors and where you are placing focus on new areas for development. Keep an archive of your maxims. Each piece of paper is a snapshot in time of your leadership philosophy. When you conduct your semiannual or annual review of your maxims, look at old versions to get a sense for how much you have grown.

You must put your maxims into practice if you want to get the benefits of the approach. Building them into your regular routines will solidify them in your mind and make it more likely that you will evaluate your behaviors and decisions against the standards your maxims represent. The more frequently you refer to them, the more naturally they will become a part of how you lead. As you grow, expect your maxims to change and grow with you. By evaluating them a few times a year or at turning points in your life, you can ensure that they stay relevant and continue to push you to grow as a person and as a leader.

CHAPTER 24

[**SHARING**]

llow me to congratulate you. You have done something special. It
is difficult to embark on the path of introspection. We are all
flawed and have things we do not like about ourselves. I have never
met anyone who did not want to change something about who she or
he was. The fact that you have taken on the challenge of exploring who
you are and who you want to be puts you in some pretty rare company.
But your work isn't over.

It is great for you to have your maxims to refer to. I am sure you
will do a wonderful job of writing them and reviewing them on a regular
basis. If you have been honest with yourself in writing them, and if you
are honest with yourself as you go through the process of evaluating
your behavior and performance against them, you will experience
positive behavior changes.

But sometimes you cannot trust yourself. You might seek to avoid
owning up to your mistakes. I know I do. You might not judge your
behavior as harshly as it needs to be judged. You might miss behaviors
that are not consistent with your maxims because said behaviors are in
your "blind spots." What is a leader to do?

Share.

THE IMPORTANCE OF SHARING

Share your maxims with others who are interested in your development and growth. Share them with people who care about you. Share them with those who want to help you be a better leader and a better person. Share them with your team and your boss. Your family and friends.

When you think about who you are going to share your maxims with, choose people who are close enough to know you well. Pick individuals with whom you interact on a regular enough basis that they can watch your behaviors change over time. Choose those individuals who are willing to commit the time and effort required to understand you, provide you with feedback, and help you grow. I know—it's awkward. I am asking you to share your beliefs and past experiences with people who might not know these things about you, and this can feel unfamiliar and risky. What you must realize is that opening up to those you work with establishes trust at a new level. You are also giving them the tools to help you along your journey to become the best leader you can be.

Sharing your maxims provides those around you with a window into who you are as a person and as a leader. By sharing your personal story, which includes both things you are proud of and things you are not, you are implicitly saying *I trust you to accept me for who I am and to not judge me for my actions and beliefs.*

Sharing your maxims is a major step in building relationships. Imagine that you are a new hire and your leader shares her maxims with you. How would you feel? You would be off to a great start in terms of knowing your leader as a person and understanding her standards and values. This act of sharing is a core step of the leadership maxims process.

HOW TO SHARE

When you share your maxims with your team members, do not simply email or copy your one piece of paper and distribute it without further context. Instead, have either a team meeting or one-on-one conversations with your people. Tell them you want to share your leadership philosophy with them. Explain how that philosophy encompasses the four aspects of leadership (leading yourself, leading the thinking, leading your people, and leading a balanced life). Share the process you went through to generate your maxims, and help them understand how you used your personal story to define your leadership philosophy. Make it clear that your maxims are your standards and expectations not only for yourself but for them as well. Talk through each maxim and share the story behind it. Let them know who you truly are as a person. I think you will be pleasantly surprised with how warmly your story will be received.

Once they have heard your story, allow them to ask questions about it. Help them understand how your maxims will be applied to everyday situations. Perhaps give them examples of recent events or hypothetical work scenarios and then explain how a particular maxim might guide your behavior in that situation. When they see how you will apply your maxims to situations they are familiar with, you become more predictable for them. As you finish this conversation, make it clear you will be using your maxims every day.

INVITE FEEDBACK

Set the expectation that your team should become familiar with your maxims and should seek clarification if they see you make a decision that is inconsistent with those maxims. There might be a good reason you have seemed to deviate from a maxim. You might be making that decision based on one maxim while they are evaluating that decision based on another. Explain and clarify that conflict for them so they better understand your decision-making process. It could be that you have indeed made a decision that conflicts with a maxim. If you have failed to live up to that maxim, it is a great opportunity to admit your shortcoming and either rectify it or resolve to behave better in the future. Take your feedback positively—and thank those who point out your inconsistencies. Yes, these conversations will be painful, but out of this pain comes growth.

Just as your team members should hold you accountable for behaving in accordance with your maxims, you must hold them accountable as well. Your maxims are your standards and values as a leader. If any of your team members do something inconsistent with the behaviors you desire, remind them of the standard you set with a particular maxim. I have had team members come into my office to discuss a particular issue and my sole response to their comments was pointing to one of my maxims on my one piece of paper. When they read the maxim (which had been explained to them in depth before), they immediately understood what I wanted them to do in that particular situation. My maxims became shorthand we used when communicating with one another. Using my maxims also reinforced the point that I expected them to live up to consistent and easily understood standards.

Try to establish the same dynamic with members of your team. Look for opportunities to give guidance or make decisions and explain how a particular maxim is relevant to the choice you are making. The more frequently you do this, the faster your team will adopt the behaviors you desire. If you are consistent in this approach, your maxims will come to life before your eyes. They will become the underlying philosophy that forms and influences the culture of your team. When that happens, you will find everyone pulling together and moving in the same direction. Talk about alignment!

Be sure you also share your maxims with your boss, peers, and business partners as appropriate. They too can give you feedback when they see you doing something inconsistent with your maxims—or praise you when they see you living out your maxims. Sharing your maxims with them involves them in your development and helps you demonstrate the behaviors you have stated you value. Additionally, these people can provide you with suggestions on how to improve your maxims. They may even provide you with new maxims you may want to adopt as your own. As you've seen, I have adopted many a maxim from those who have led me.

NEXT STEPS

Encourage everyone—your team members, peers, bosses, and other colleagues—to go through the process of creating their own set of personal leadership maxims. Give them a copy of this book as a gift and encourage them to join the Leadership Maxims online community (more on this follows). Once they have created their own set of maxims, help them live up to the standards on their one piece of paper. Give them coaching and feedback to help them achieve the behavioral changes they are seeking to make.

You can try to do this on your own, but the process will be infinitely easier, more enjoyable, and more effective when you connect with others from the outset. To successfully craft and, more important, put into practice your leadership maxims, I urge you to involve others in the process. To this end, I have created another resource for you beyond this book. At www.onepieceofpaper.com you will find a forum for sharing your maxims, stories, suggestions, and ideas with other like-minded leaders. In the forums you can share your maxims, tell the stories behind them, read other peoples' maxims and stories, and engage in conversations about leadership with other great leaders. I will also regularly update the site with new articles and videos about leadership, suggestions on other great leadership resources, and responses to your maxims and stories. A friend of mine always says "Iron sharpens iron." I invite you to come get sharpened in the leadership maxims community.

Leadership is intensely personal. You have to put your whole person into it. Leadership philosophies are individual statements that define how one person functions as a leader. They should not conform to some cookie-cutter mold. They do not have to be long or full of buzzwords and bullshit. In fact, they must be the exact opposite to be authentic and practical. There is no "textbook solution" leadership philosophy. The only thing that authentic, practical leadership philosophies have in common is the approach to creating them. That approach must be comprehensive and cover the leader's entire experience—not just who the leader is at work. The leadership maxims approach is designed to provide you with a holistic framework that results in the creation of your unique leadership philosophy. It is *your* philosophy—your one piece of paper—that will help you connect with your teams and lead your people in a manner that enables you to be the leader you always knew you could be.

ACKNOWLEDGMENTS

It amazes me how many people I have had the wonderful fortune of knowing and who have enriched and improved my life in immeasurable ways. Without these folks, the wonderful life I live would not be possible. Without these people, I would be devoid of many of the insights and ideas I have shared in this book. This book itself would not be possible without their efforts and their fanatical support of my endeavors. I am compelled to publicly thank these people for all they have done for me. They have made me the leader and person I am today. I am eternally grateful, and I hope I can repay their kindness, love, and support in some way in the future. I am sure I will miss some people in this list, and for that I am profoundly sorry. It isn't personal. I'm just getting old.

To Amy. I would not be here without you. Thank you for your love, courage, patience, cheerleading, and tireless support of all I do. Thank you for helping me through dark and troubling times and for being by my side as we've enjoyed the bright ones. I am sorry for the times I have let you down and thankful for the times you have helped me through incredible pain, fear, and uncertainty. I love you tremendously.

To Danielle, Michael, and Alexandra. You are three priceless blessings in my life. Thank you for brightening my day, giving me perspective, loving me unconditionally, and reminding me what is important in life. I hope at some point in your lives you find this book helpful in guiding you and helping you navigate the challenges and opportunities in your futures. I love you guys immeasurably.

To Mom and Dad. Thank you for your love, never-ending support, guidance, and willingness to push me to be more than I ever dreamed I could. You guys gave me so many gifts, one of which is the "original" set of maxims for me to live by. I love both of you for all you have done and continue to do for me and my family.

To my other Mom and Dad. Thank you for welcoming me into your family and for loving me as your own son. Your support, love, and kindness is appreciated more than you know.

To Gina, Andy, and Jaylene. What a fantastic group of siblings. Thank you for the laughs, the support, and the love.

To my grandparents. I love all of you and miss those of you no longer with us more than you can imagine. You have had a huge positive impact on my life, and I hope I have made you proud of what I have become.

To J. and T. You two saved my life. Thank you.

To Rich Santoli, Bucky Rehain, Ron Angello, Pete Gruttadauria, Bob Coyne, Bob Buccino, and Ken Foley. You guys kicked my ass on the wrestling mat and the soccer field and made me a better person for it. Thanks for never taking it easy on me, always believing in me, and helping me believe in myself even in the face of adversity.

To Mr. Shreve, Mr. Jordan, Mrs. Morgan, Mrs. Luft, Mr. Wachtel, Mr. Osburn, Mrs. Demora, Mr. Hansen, Mr. Toigo, Miss LaBella, Mrs. Clemen, Mrs. Joseph, Mr. Hollis, Mr. Gabrielson, Mrs. Sonnie, Mr. Snell, Mr. Tusch, Mr. Hageman, Mr. Lewinter, and every other teacher who has suffered through having me in your classroom. Thank you for your dedication to learning, education, and my development. While I may not have appreciated your efforts while I was in class, I am eternally grateful for all you taught me, now that I understand the gifts you were giving me every day.

To Ty, Bill, Andy, Thu, Joseph, Noah, Mike, Rich, Sonki, and Sean. You guys were the greatest friends and roommates ever. I could not have made it through that place without you. Thanks for all the laughs, help, support, and unconditional friendship. You guys are the brothers I never had. I will never forget all the things you did for me. Start the days!

To COL Black, GEN Galvin, CPT Masiello, MAJ Sole, LTC Hennelly, MAJ Hayes, MAJ Toguchi, LTC Norton, MAJ Mitchell, MAJ Holtzclaw, MAJ Gray, MAJ Gruner, COL Walker, Dr. McMullen, MAJ Hahn, MAJ Perwich, and every other West Point instructor I had the honor and pleasure of learning from. Your selfless service, wisdom, knowledge, honor, and teaching ability gave me more than I ever dreamed I could get in four years. You have left a powerful, positive, indelible mark on my life, and I am eternally grateful for your hard work, dedication, patience, and guidance.

To CPT Evan Brown (yes I know you've been promoted since then, but my thanks are for the time I served you as a captain). You taught me what it means to stand up for your people. You created an environment where I could fail (often) and learn. You were an infinitely patient, fiercely loyal, and wonderful friend. Thank you for being a role model for how a great leader should lead his people.

To SFC Laloulu, SSG Curtis, SSG Smith, SSG Gear, SGT Villarreal, and the rest of 2nd Platoon, Delta Company, 2–77 Armor. I am proud to have served with you. You guys taught me how to be a "soldier's officer." It was my honor to serve you and call you "my soldiers." I would do anything for you guys, and I know you would do the same for me. Thanks for keeping me safe and for always making me look good. You embodied the philosophy of talk softly but carry a 120 mm cannon.

To Dave McCormick, Gunjan Kedia, Steve Schwarzwaelder, Steve Delity, Kevin Berner, John Stoner, Cecilia Frew, Duncan Gillis, Narendra Bhat, Anjan Asthana, Martin Barkman, Maia Hansen, Mac Harman, Shubham Singhal, Katie Liebel, Lawrence Wood, Mukund

Vasudevan, Tom Corpus, Paul Mango, Carl Mays, Joe Martin, Chris Leech, Tim Chapman, Luis Troyano, Mike Longman, Peter Simon, Julian McCarthy, and all my other McKinsey colleagues. You folks are the smartest people I have ever met. You made me one thousand times smarter than the day I walked in the door. Thank you for teaching me, pushing me, and giving me second, third, and fourth chances, and for providing me countless tools for how to successfully run a business. I appreciate your professionalism, your friendship, and the example you've set for me.

To Terry Edwards, Paul Zamecnik, Ryan Schneider, Eric Nelson, Mark Schwartz, Joe Petite, and Tim Portland. You guys were wonderful to work for. You taught me more than you can ever imagine. I enjoyed the great times with you, and I appreciate the difficult times. I know things were not always perfect. I respect you as professionals and for how you handled everything that came your way. Thank you for all the time and effort you invested in me. I am a better leader and person for all of it.

To all the folks who have ever been a member of one of my teams. Wow. It is a true honor and privilege to have worked with you. You impressed me with your skills, and I am excessively proud of your achievements. I know I was not always the best leader. I know I outright failed on many occasions. Thank you for the opportunity you gave me to lead you. I can only hope I gave you one one-hundredth of the things my leaders gave me. Thank you for your loyalty, hard work, dedication, and friendship.

To Alan Veeck, Dave Willis, Jarrod Spencer, Maureen Metcalf, Belinda Gore, Jack Maher, Mike Lynn, Brian Link, Mike Sheehan, Andy Hohman, Todd Miller, Scott Wielar, Nick Seguin, and Brian Ahearn. You folks are the best business partners I could ever ask for. Thank you for your support, guidance, ideas, cheerleading, friendship, and loyalty. I could never do the things I do without you folks.

To my clients, Gail, Sheri, Marlon, Amy, Mark, Lois, Lesli, Lynn, Vildan, Jill, Mark, MaryBeth, Craig, Chris, Kim, Lori, Christophe, Lisa, Amy, Marcella, Darcie, Leah, Kim, Ed, Jim, Ursula, Rick, Cecilia,

Tim, Pam, Lee, Kathy, Kristina, Kim, Andy, Gunjan, Phil, Mike, Nick, Andrew, Brad, Thom, Dale, Josh, Steve, David, Ram, and everyone else who has ever sat in one of my classrooms or spent time working with me. You have no idea what your support means to me. You enable me to live my dream every day. The trust you place in me to teach your people is an honor, and I truly treasure it. Your partnership and friendship is one of the most valuable assets of my business. I hope I live up to my promise to make you look brilliant when you bring me and my team in to work in your organizations. Thank you for all you have done and continue to do for me.

To Mary Ellen Slayter and the SmartBrief team. Thank you for shining a spotlight on my work and for spreading my ideas around the world. You are directly responsible for this book being possible. Thank you for your support, friendship, and partnership, and for the countless opportunities you create for me.

To Giles Anderson of the Anderson Literary Agency. Thank you for searching in interesting places to find new authors. Your guidance and coaching through the entire process of getting this thing published has been invaluable. Thank you for helping make a longtime dream of mine come true. I can only hope I have delivered a work that meets your expectations. Thanks for opening the door to this opportunity for me.

To Karen Murphy and the Jossey-Bass team. Thank you for giving me the chance to get this message out there. I hope all the effort I put into this work is evidence of how much I appreciate the opportunity you have given me.

To anyone I missed. Thank you. I'm sorry my old age is making my memory fuzzy.

The names I've used in the stories in this book have been changed to respect people's privacy and some of the stories are composites of individuals and companies I have worked with.

APPENDIX A: THE AUTHOR'S MAXIMS

On the following page are my leadership maxims. They have changed over time. Some of the maxims listed there have been removed from my list or replaced as I have grown. I am always searching for new maxims and ways to articulate my approach to leadership. You should be prepared to approach this process the same way. Maxims are a living document to be shared, reviewed, and practiced regularly. Note—although some of these maxims have been "retired," they occasionally come out of retirement for special engagements as necessary.

Leading Yourself

Light bulbs

He never stopped learning, teaching, and coaching.

What would Nana say?

It's hard to shave if you can't look yourself in the mirror.

It is what it is. What are you going to do about it?

"But man is not made for defeat. A man can be destroyed but not defeated."

I see it, I own it.

Leading the Thinking

In God we trust. All others bring data.

A cadet will not lie, cheat, or steal nor tolerate those who do.

Is this right for the customer?

To become a global firm of uniquely skilled executives who teach managers around the world how to be great leaders.

Why? Why? Why? Why? Why?

So what? So what? So what? So what? So what? So what? So what?

"If you choose not to decide you still have made a choice."

"In case of doubt, attack!"

Leading Your People

Kick up. Kiss down.

Don't bring me problems. Bring me solutions.

You have two ears and one mouth for a reason.

He drinks 7UP.

"He's under the tank, sir."

"But he's never done that job!"

It's easier to correct course 100 yards into the journey than 100 miles into it.

Leading a Balanced Life

"I'm going home. You're doing my job."

Burger King is hiring.

A Burger King crown

It's only [blank].

A bad day of fishing is better than a good day of work.

APPENDIX B: YOUR MAXIMS

Use these pages to capture the first draft of your leadership maxims. When you are satisfied with this draft, transfer them to your computer and put them on one piece of paper.

Leading Yourself

Why do you get out of bed every day?

How will you shape your future?

What guidelines do you live by?

When you fall down, how do you pick yourself back up?

How do you hold yourself accountable?

Leading the Thinking

What standards do you hold your team to?

Where are you taking your people?

How will you foresee the future?

After all that thinking, how will you drive action?

Leading Your People

What is your natural style?

How will you remember to treat your team members as individuals?

How will you stay connected to your team's reality?

How will you commit to your people's growth?

Leading a Balanced Life

How will you define your boundaries?

How will you keep things in perspective?

What are you passionate about?

ABOUT THE AUTHOR

Mike Figliuolo is an honor graduate of the United States Military Academy at West Point, where he graduated in the top 5 percent of his class. He served in the U.S. Army as an armor officer. After several years of leading soldiers in the army, Mike spent time in corporate America as a consultant at McKinsey & Company and as an executive in various roles at Capital One Financial and the Scotts Miracle-Gro Company.

Mike is the founder and managing director of *thought*LEADERS, LLC (www.thoughtleadersllc.com). He and his team train senior executives at leading companies on topics of leadership, strategy, communications, and innovation. A highly sought-after speaker and trainer, Mike has delivered his message to thousands of executives and leaders through keynote presentations, classroom instruction, and personal coaching.

Mike's clients include Abbott Laboratories, Discover Financial Services, Heinz, Oracle, Cardinal Health, the Federal Reserve Bank, Bain Capital, Nationwide, ServiceMASTER, and many other industry-leading firms.

INDEX